Paul Bunyan

Paul Bunyan
Larry Beckett

Smokestack Books
1 Lake Terrace, Grewelthorpe, Ripon HG4 3BU
e-mail: info@smokestack-books.co.uk
www.smokestack-books.co.uk

ISBN 978-0-9929581-7-6

Smokestack Books is represented
by Inpress Ltd

1

Out of the wild North woods, in the thick of the timber
And through the twirling of the winter of the blue snow,
Within an inch of sunup, with the dream shift ending,
A man mountain, all hustle, all muscle and bull bones,
An easy winner, full of swagger, a walking earthquake,
A skyscraper, looking over the tallest American tree,
A smart apple, a wonder inventor, the sun's historian,
A cock-a-doodle hero, a hobo, loud, shrewd, brawling,
Rowdy, brash as the earth, stomping, big-hearted, raw,
Paul Bunyan lumbered and belly-laughed back at the stars.
He was rigged out in a slouch hat, a red work shirt
Under his faithful mackinaw with its hickory buttons,
Suspenders and high-water stag pants, which were tucked
Into his brass-hooked and buckskin-laced black boots,
And this foot-loose blue ox was sashaying at his side:
Babe, who was combed with a garden rake, who measured
Exactly forty-two ax handles and a plug of Star tobacco
Between the eyes, who was crazy for parsnips, who ate
And just bellowed for joy, his bray rocking the country,
And who romped off the deer path, skylarking, and leaving
The thousand and one hoof prints which are now Maine lakes.
Out of the scud covering up the dusty morning stars,
The baby-blue snowflakes of the first blue snowfall
Were scurrying down sky-blue, all over, like butterflies,
In flurries, blue as Monday, blue as the moon, as heaven,
Decorating the pines, blue as a ribbon, blue as bluegrass,
As blue songs and blue laws, and glittering on the boughs
Like jays and berries: it was icing up the evergreens,
Sticking to itself, and stacking in balls and drifts
Like fury, and the seconds were as tight as the icicles;
It was quiet like it's quiet before the sour beginning
Of the redbreast's la-de-dah, and in that minute there
All of a sudden Paul Bunyan itched for big-time work.
He uprooted a tree, combed the frost out of his beard,
Rolling fifty-two notions around his burning head
Till it all flashed on him, and he invented logging!
He whistled and walked over to the local iron range,
Fixed up a blade, fit on a white pine for a handle,
And jogged back with his ax: he carved himself a gabriel
Out of a cedar, lifted up the horn and let out a honk
Whinnying from the Rockies all around to the Rockies

Like day breaking; and when the wide yellow sun rose,
Old Paul braced and, taking a colossal breath, he roared,
'Roll out or roll up, boys; there's daylight in the swamp!'
All this ruckus was to bounce lumberjacks everywhere
Out of bed, and between the horn and the ballyhoo
His boys woke up. While the man power was on the way,
He sized up the eastern timber, and scribbled a claim:
He spit into his broad palms and circled his ax back,
Leaned like a natural into his swing, and every whack
He grunted like he was happy, chopping into this tree
So thick a man might sprint round it in a day, so tall
It'd take a week to see its top up in the clouds;
When the big stick was whittled on down to a whistle,
It crackled, it swished, it got the shivers in its limbs,
And when it snapped, it tilted, timber splintered, twigs
All tore off, and it rip-roared down in green confusion.
Babe tagged behind Paul, chawing off the little branches
And hauling out the logs; and to level out the country,
Bunyan strung up the stumps in chains, to an iron spool,
And hitched it to Babe, who jerked them free and lugged
The breaking plow, which had a huge furrow, and filled in
The hollows, and they cleared hundreds of acres, easy.
Old Paul scrawled the plans for the shanties on the air
And plunked the logs crisscross for walls, jacking roof poles
And trueing them, checking out his plans, slapping up shingles
In dovetailing and overlapping style against the rain
In fog so heavy he nailed six feet of shingles on it,
And for his big finish to this bang-up job, he squatted
On the roofs and welded the timber as tight as anything.
Now all the burly, joking, gallivanting lumberjacks
Showed up and rolled in, sailing, thumbing, and hiking,
Foreigners out of the old countries, and talking funny,
Like Limeys, Micks, Frogs, Canucks, and Scandihoovians,
And Yankee Doodle boys hailing from the four corners
Of the United States, Fly-up-the-creeks from Florida,
Evergreen men from Washington, Pine tree men from Maine,
California Golden Bears, with Corn Crackers, Knickerbockers,
Granite Boys, Green Mountain Boys, Old Liners, Old Colonials,
Buckeyes, Muskrats, Panhandlers, Mudcats, Yellowhammers,
Hardheads, Sandhillers, Tarheels, from down East and Dixie,
An all-star team, and the ruggedest crew ever crowed:

Wrestlers, wreckers, boozers, barnstormers, roustabouts,
Breadwinners, ramblers, fiddlers, roughnecks, runaways,
Penpushers, windjammers, daredevils, and crackhunters,
And no galoot in the whole gang under eight feet tall,
Come in with a caterwaul to join Paul Bunyan's camp
On the river and kick off the original lumber drive.
The camp sprawled from the Smiling River to Honey Creek
Sunning and curling around the Big Rock Candy Mountain,
Where the strawberry bushes, where the raspberry trees
All ran wild on the slopes with berries as big as plums
By the plash and swizzle of the rock-and-rye springs,
Under the gillygaloo, which brooded up on the steep
Of Pyramid Forty, with its stand of one million pines,
And laid square eggs which wouldn't roll down the hill
And when collected and hard-boiled were good for dice,
And way over behind beyond, the whangdoodle whistled.
Down in the bottom lands below Honey Creek, in soil
As smooth as butter, old Paul's dairy farm spread out
Like paradise, where the wheat was growing in fields
So thick the geography just creaked under the weight,
The corn so quick a crack logger couldn't hit it twice
In the same for heaven's sake spot, and where sting bees
The size of doves went whizzing into the tall dandelions,
Where the red clover cows gave milk that didn't sour
And the devil grass cows gave straight cough medicine,
Where the green vegetables were rooted so god-awful deep
It took an inventor to pick them, and where a redneck
One day chanced to see sparrowgrass sprout up so hard
It went roots and all into the air, and lived on nothing
But the climate, and he saw vines dragging punkins along,
And when he got tangled up, he went for his jackknife
And found a big cowcumber that had ripened in his pocket.
When Pea Soup Shorty clattered the triangle for breakfast,
The boys stampeded for the cookshack and grabbed up forks
At a pine table so long a story started up at one end
Was so tall at the other end they had to hire a flunky
To shovel it out the door. Now first off, and for starters,
There was oatmeal mush, logging berries, hasty pudding,
Eggs fried over easy, over hard, sourdough biscuits,
Klondike spuds, pilgrim marbles, apple grunt, sowbelly,
With all the trimmings, and a gallon of bullshit a man:

When they rolled sugar cookies down the table the boys
At the foot got gypped, and so Big Ole the blacksmith
Dreamed up the hole and toted the doughnuts on a stick.
All this was only horse ovaries before the main dish:
Hotcakes! They had a choice between pancakes, flatcakes,
Slapjacks, griddlecakes, stovelids, battercakes, flapjacks,
In piles, topped with skid grease, floating in maple slick.
The iron griddle, one hundred yards wide, over a fire
Kindled out of an acre of scrub and two of timber,
Was oiled up by kids who strapped on slabs of bacon
And skated across: out of sugar boxes, flour barrels,
Crates of rooster's eggs and a fancy dairy the cook
Conjured up the batter in a bucket big as a steamboat,
Which was hoisted up and tipped over, creating puddles
On the stove, and he used popcorn to flip the flapcakes
To the waiters, who were on roller skates to go faster.
The boys dove into the breakfast like wildcats, chomping
And slurping with a noise like Niagara, and they busted
Out the door into the frosty camp, with the raw sun
In the east sky, all rosy on the froth of the river,
And the waking up pines stinking up the air real pretty,
And Paul Bunyan standing out on American mud, ready
To big-talk to his bunch of drifters, and brag up logging:
'It's an okay morning, boys, and it's good to breathe:
This country's lucky, and so splendiferous you want
Oh, to cartwheel and kick your initials in the sky,
Spread-eagle, hug the whole territory for dear love,
Whoop hallelujah just to hear your god-damn voice,
And reel off here and yonder with a square dance heart!
I swear only a yellowbelly or a lazybones could go
And let this morning slide, and keep from sinking steel
Into white pine, but it's obvious as a mockingbird
We can't scatter like a mess of kids out of school
Or we'll wind up with nothing but a little sawdust;
All right, so slack up a minute and promise with me
On the river, your bible, to go by the logger's rules.
One, always talk straight; be bald-faced, stick to it
Like it was old whiskey: I hear of a man dealing
In a double-talking lie, I'll hang up his ax myself.
I don't mean you can't story, now; I've been fishing
And I like to stretch it for fun, but it's the fakes
And the horse traders, the two timers I'm against.

Two, there's no brawling and no boozing in the woods:
I might see a little back-of-the-shanty roughhousing,
Or a short nip on a cold Sunday, and turn my head,
But when your drunk or free-for-all holds up the drive
By a wink, say goodbye to your pals, because you're gone.
Three, if you drag yourself to the city come spring
I want you to be all slow fingers and sweet talk
With the fillies. I imagine your idea is belly bumping,
Which is wonderful, but I catch you beating on a woman,
Look out: whatever you give her I'm going to give you.
Okay, boys, speak up; you're on your own say-so, here:
I need upwards of half of you as sawyers, to fall
The trees, whirling an ax sharp as sunlight around you
Till you steam, and ache all over, till your veins bulge;
I need plenty of swampers, to bust up the scenery,
And slash and rut the trails, and to lop off the limbs
From the down pine, which calls for backbone and stay;
And I need ox-strong skidders, to tug the logs to sleighs
And snake the load across the ice, over the toteroad
On down to the rollway, on the slopes of the branch;
And at the spring breakup I need the top lumberjacks
As the water rats, who'll ride the logs down the river
Into the snags and jams, just for the glory of it.
Now take a breath of this almighty Appalachian air,
Grin like an old pioneer, and pitch into the timber!'

2

Winter broke out in the up country with a big bang
And a big wind, blowing all morning without a letup,
Wheezing like a harmonium, whooping through the boughs
Of the stiff pines, squabbling with itself, puffing so hard
It tossed rocks like kisses, ripped holes out of the ground,
It hit an old black bear in the mouth and it whisked him
Inside out, it squashed the clouds, it snatched the feathers
Off the chickens and stuck them on the ever-loving hogs,
It leaned everything east, and tried to bully the sun.
There was a log chain hanging from the roof of a shanty
For a wind gauge: if it rattled it meant it was breezy,
If it was swinging, it was real windy, if it laid out flat,
It was a gale, and it was floating off into the blue.
This wind was cuckoo; it'd blow up, blow down, and
Then it'd stand still and blow six ways from Sunday;
It was kind of like the weather in the big timber days,
And the balled up seasons when the calendar got knocked
Out of whack: a haywire spring, oh maybe a winter,
A screwball fall, a buffalo summer rolled in at random,
Nothing took turns, and after, say a couple of summers
And no spring, or a month with four seasons squeezed in,
The almanacs took up comedy, and the weather prophets
Went south. This foolishness was foxing Paul Bunyan,
Who was up to here in his ledgers, logging the logging,
Who, with such-and-such receivables, so-and-so payables,
His red invoices, his black bills, his ice cream payroll, was
Writing his chronicles, and book-balancing like an acrobat.
He got blisters on all of his fingers counting up like so:
One horse, two bits, three cheers, four stars, five fingers,
Six shooter, seven natural, eight ball, nine day wonder,
Ten gallon hat, start over. He set his green fountain pen
Down on his desk, rubbing his face to wake up, snarling:
'Oh man, I'm tired of this god-almighty paper work!
I'm liable to squat and bust if I can't hit my old woods;
My boys are breathing hard, falling the ponderosa, yeah
And I sit here doodling, tuckered out by the numbers.
I'll bet they're goofing up without a straw boss there,
But how can I be the man when I'm totally swamped
By accounts? I'm missing the whole hoot owl morning!
I add up the figures, but all I get is one more figure,
And it's not like I don't look for short cuts, but hell,

I calculated with both hands, and I just got woozy;
I gave the boys a pop quiz to see who might spell me
And graded it on a curve, but ha! everybody flunked;
I called up a gang to carve my arithmetic on trees,
I'd holler out three numbers at once, they'd screw up,
And when I lost track of them, I scrapped the idea;
I invented logarithms, which was natural, but it seems
My characteristic was always fouled up in my mantissa,
And I'd monkey with it so long I wasn't saving time;
I don't know, I guess I'm just bound to let a foreman
Go and crack the whip, while I wrestle with the math.'
The original push Paul signed on was Shot Gunderson,
The iron eater, the bear tamer, the all-creation hunter,
The rip-snorting snuff chewer, who could knock a cougar
Spang out of a bull pine with one good tobacco squirt.
He was a big noise on account of his mouth thunder,
And he was a slam-down jack-up bawl-out old bastard
Who might reel it off for days, like a one-man riot,
And it's said he could cuss the quills off a porcupine.
One time all his curses were written down in a book
Called The Ox-Skinner's Dictionary, but it burned up,
And the story goes it was by spontaneous combustion.
Shot Gunderson was breaking in his highball system
On the Tadpole River, up in the Bullfrog Lake country,
And he was croaking so loud into this absurd wind
His voice cracked up into nothing, into a squeak,
And without his old thunder it was goodbye job, but
Shot's back talk had caught on real glorious with the boys,
And from that day on lumberjacks used flowery lingo.
The new foreman was punch-drunk Chris Crosshaul, who
Was a white water maniac and loved to ride the logs
With a hundred-damn-verse song, and a fanatic smile,
And who hustled the timber down White River, rolling
By the unreal badlands, and right on past the town,
Which obliged the river pigs to drive it back upstream
In an upstream drive, an immortal rough grind
Which winded them, when Paul fed Babe a sack of salt
And had the blue ox slurp water till the river reversed.
Old Paul sent this bad character back to the swamp
Without a farewell party, and kept his ear on his boys:
'Hey tenderfoot, look out!' 'You talking to me, fool?'

'I don't see nobody else.' 'I didn't hear you say sir.'
'I was wondering if you saw the black hodag go by you.'
'What on earth's a black hodag?' 'Oh, it's a thing that feeds
On mud turtles, water snakes, muskrats, and human beans;
It's like a rooster with steel feathers which it can throw
With dead aim; it was right behind you, and you missed it.'
'I was too busy watching the luferlang in your tree.'
'Now don't you josh me, kid.' 'Oh yeah, it's triple-jointed
And dark-striped, and it's got a fox tail. I understand
It'll attack you for nothing, and if it bites you, bang!
You're on ice. It eats you and it's harmless all year.'
'I guess it ain't hungry. Hey, what's this about a pilgrim?'
'The word is a Swedish mountain man, big as Bunyan,
And with a razzle-dazzle style, is coming to the camp.'
'Oh mama, what was that, an earthquake or something?'
'I believe it's walking!' 'I'll be –' 'Hey, hold on, man!'
Big Swede, the bull of the woods, was swaggering up
Out of nowhere, sure as Shenandoah, yellow-haired,
Sky-tall and red-faced, grinning his great buck teeth,
His eyes blue fight, and his big paws jammed in his pockets.
Old Paul looked, but he didn't need a barber to tell him
This was his foreman: he walked over to say howdy
And it felt funny, because it was his first handshake.
His new old friend greeted everybody with a yawp:
'Welcome! Hello, boys. Good morning, I'm Big Swede!
I come from Sweden. I'm over here in America now.
I was walking on the mountains. I heard of logging.
This is the job for me, I said. This is a lot of fun.
This beats walking on the mountains. Oh, I sailed away!
I crossed the puddle in between us, I mean the Atlantic.
I work like a mule, but I'm better. I don't wear out.
I'm with you guys, if it's all right. There is one hitch:
I don't take baths. I don't like water. I'll wash up
On January one. Okay? Happy new year! Thanks.'
Old Paul got thick with Big Swede, and after a little
Back slapping and joke swapping, he rallied the camp:
'Way out yonder in the grand frontier Dakota country
And somewhere from the Souris to the Cheyenne River
Is the mountain that stands on its head, like an upside
Down miracle, steep as a winter moon, and miles high.
Its peak's stuck in the ground, and on its green slopes

The timber grows down, all the creeks run backwards,
And flittericks, the flying squirrels, go zooming, quick
As cannon balls, in barrel rolls, lazy eights, loop the loops:
Its foot's a flat I don't exactly know how wide, and
Up there the springs are burbling, and the phillyloo bird,
With a big beak like a stork and no feathers to spare,
Sails with its belly up to the sun to ward off colds.
Buck up, you hayseeds, I want you to log this mountain:
It's an out-and-out dare to a real lumberjack, boys,
And on top of that it'll make my chronicles look good.
Whether you walk turvy-topsy or up on your hands
Is Big Swede's business, I'm signing him as your push.
Okay now, everybody scream hurray, and go to work!'
Big Swede and the boys waded into the green trees,
Hooting like indians, and high-stepping over the weeds,
While Paul kicked a pine cone, and slunk into his office.
First off, they logged in the lowlands, whopping so fast
They took time outs to cool their broadaxes in the river,
And the hurricane work went just as nice as whiskey,
Outside of the trouble of keeping all the axes sharp:
The old method was to kick a boulder off a hill
And run like hell beside it while holding out the ax
And letting it scrape till it was all honed and true,
And so Bunyan invented the grindstone out of mercy.
Big Swede hustled lumberjacks between woods and camp,
And after hollering for the get-up-and-go shift
He took them on the quiet to tackle the mountain,
Without a word, let alone a huddle, with old Paul,
Who was left behind with his approaches on paper,
And who shook his head over it, but let the slap go.
By and by the first men trudged back, all washed out,
And Big Swede, a little frazzled, with a blank eye,
Rousted another crew and headed out to the mountain.
The lumber output dwindled down to splinters and chips,
And so Paul dropped everything to go out for a looksee:
Big Swede had lashed these cables from trunk to trunk,
From which, upside down and by tight timber hitches,
All of the swampers and sawyers were hanging, hooked,
Dizzy and red, with the dirt and sawdust in their eyes,
And their caps, pipes and flasks tumbling away for miles,
While Big Swede honked and yammered, wheedling the men:

'Yikes! We've got a goose egg, here! Why won't you, now?
Look, if you chop the trees I'll give you a big surprise;
If you don't chop I'll knock all your heads together!
Why don't you chop the trees? This is Big Swede talking:
Oh come on, you can do it, I say you can! You can't.
Hold on, boys! We've got axes and ropes, what's wrong?
We've got a bum mountain. Mister Bunyan's loony. Aw!'
Paul rambled back for his old double-barrel shotgun,
Which was so big that when it was busted and he used
Its barrels for the smokestacks of the first sawmill,
They were so tall they were hinged to let the clouds go by:
He had Big Ole the blacksmith make outlandish bullets
Out of brass-bound and sheet iron-capped cedar logs,
While the boys walked in, bitched, buggered, and bewildered,
Winking their eyes, too blown to go back to the mountain;
And when Big Swede shrugged his broad-beam shoulders and
Said the mountain was too many for him and move on,
Old Paul spit and reddened, stamped on his heel and roared.
Now he had three voices: first, his snort, inside a room,
Was gracious, like a sea breeze, just a curl in the air;
Second, in the great outdoors, his yell was a living gale;
And third, his roar was so loud it would light a fire
In the woods and snuff it, like he boomed this morning:
'Damn you good-for-nothing saps, where in hell are your balls,
You dumb jackass dimwit thickskull lunkhead greenhorn
All thumbs chicken-heart weak-knee baby-face oafs?
What kind of wag-tail sissies are you, you milkmaids?
Mom's calling, you bums, go home: you're so lackadaisical,
Hey! you couldn't cut down a daffodil with a ripsaw!
Do you imagine a sea dog quits it just because he's
Sailing in the wind's eye? No, man: he trims his canvas
And scuds close-hauled, and that old head wind's in his sails.
Can you see a dirt farmer just kissing his fields off
To the flood when a fence-lifting rain falls? No, man!
He slaps a dam up and wham, there's his July water.
It's just horse sense, I mean, trouble ain't trouble, see,
You big palookas, if you've got the lumberjack's eye.
Come on, Big Swede, you windbag, you all follow me;
Why, logging this upside down mountain will be easy
As blinking at the sun: you just watch a good worker.'
Out at the mountain old Paul cocked and skied his popgun,

And, jerking the trigger, shot fire out of both barrels:
It rained all kinds of rubble, and when the smoke spun off
All of the dazzled men sang whoop-de-doo to their stars,
Because the two shells had sheared off a thousand trees,
Which had dove down and become an upside down woods.
Paul Bunyan banged the trees, quick-loading, sharpshooting,
And his jacks bumped them over in a flash, in a snap,
Oh boy it was easy, and Big Swede took back charge.
Paul was slumped at his desk later on, slow figuring,
When he peeked out his window, and gawked: all of his men
Were back in camp, gabbing, lollygagging, horsing around;
He was skin-pinching amazed, and when he asked them what,
They said Big Swede decided to handle it all by himself.
Old Paul felt crazy in his belly, and a four-alarm fire
In his blood; he lit out for the mountain like a sting bee
And in no mood for a jaw session, huffing and grunting,
Whacking his hand against the air, and vowing to shape
This bull-shooting pig-feather upstart up and fast,
Before he lost his best saw boss, and all for nothing.
When he arrived at the mountain that stands on its head,
Big Swede was halfway up it, and old Paul bawled out,
'Okay, dreamer, you haul your butt back down to earth!
What's your story, huh? Why don't you let it slide? Don't
Act deaf with me, you dumb roundhead, or I'll start yelling!
I don't mind saying I'm a little perturbed with you.
Turn back, talk back, or by heaven I'll show you how!'
Big Swede wasn't speaking, the old-time mountain man
Was bouncing up the hill, rock to rock like a goat;
On top he unhitched his big ax from his studded belt
And, sizing up a stand of firs, he crowed back down:
'Oh boy, I love elbow room! Now I've got my own ax,
And my bunch of trees: this is my lumber camp, chief!
Hey, you shut up, you bag of air: don't monkey with me.
You hire me on, and what? You horn in on my job!
Yeah, I looked real dumb but, oh my rags and patches,
I'm my own big shot now, I quit: go blow your nose!'
Now old Paul's eyes were sparking, his beard was smoking:
When he sighted up the cliff, it was just too steep
And he backed up a mile for a tall-stepping jump,
Ran like a congressman, and zoomed into the blue
But missed the peak, and sprawled under his own landslide.

He spluttered onto his feet and rumbled up this hill,
And from there he jumped up skyward, lifting his arms,
And catching his fingers on the rim of the mountain.
He hauled himself up to the green flat and squawked good
As he danced in a circle, stomping, flapping his elbows
And hooting, waggling his head like a turkey, rocking
On his heels like a grizzly, till with a funny look
In his man's direction, he stood: his new foreman
Was giggling, squirting up into the air, and coming
Down in a corkscrew motion, sticking his arms out
Whirlwind style, kicking like a mule at a picnic,
Way up high, squinting into the hard winter sun,
And he only quit when he heard Paul Bunyan holler:
'Yahoo! I'm an old hawk, and I'm hungry for greenhorns!
I'm two-fisted, and inhuman is too polite! I'm full
Of prickles, and only a free-for-all will calm me down!
Oh, I'm going to surround you like a backwoods rain,
And introduce you to the stars! I'm itching for you!'
'Oh yeah? I'm scared, honey! But look out: I'm ugly,
And I love it! See, my punching bag's a beehive, ha!
And I'm all knuckles! I'm bad weather, and I hit hard!
I'll blow through you! I'm half man and I'm half hammer!
I'll pound you so flat you'll be a poster of yourself!'
'I hope you've said your goodbyes, because I'm riled now!
I swear I'll kick the shit and daylights out of you,
You big impossible cross-eyed finger-twiddling moron!
Yeah, laugh; but I'm going to knock you ass over appetite,
You stuck-up fat-headed red-necked unfaithful punk!'
'Okay, boss! But don't be so cantankerous with me,
It ain't healthy! Hey you, guess what! You're a polecat,
And you stink! Come here, my fist wants to talk to you!
When I'm all done you'll be looking for work in a circus,
You chicken, you cheat, you bluebird, you damn accountant!'
Big Swede yowled like an iron horse, and charged over,
Butting into old Paul's belly, slamming him to the grass,
Oh but Bunyan kicked him where it counts and bobbed up
Swinging, clouting the Swede in the forehead, ducking
A hook, taking a thump to the ribs, hammering back,
Old Paul was dancing, side-wheeling to his left
Around Big Swede, and biff! connecting with a jab, and wham!
Blood spouted from the Swede's eye, and with body blows

Landing, he lashed out, he was hurt, and jolted Bunyan
With a stiff counter punch, he yanked him by the whiskers
And waltzed a little with him, swiped at old Paul's chin,
Who spun off, tussling Big Swede down, where they wrangled
And slugged it out, rough-and-tumble, till they saw stars,
Big Swede on top, banging away with the old one-two,
And now it was Bunyan on top of the bucking Swede,
Walloping him pow! in the kisser with a hard right!
It was real dusty up there, and the two fist fighters,
Trading argument settlers, were wrapped up in a cloud,
It was bad, it was blue murder, the blood was flying,
The absolute booms of the jawbreaking, haymaking,
Heart-busting punches had all the bunkhouses wobbling
In the lumber camp, and the whole territory rocked.
It was a knock-down drag-out by Dakota rules:
There ain't any, and the big brawl went on for ages;
When the ruckus was over and the cloud calmed down,
The lumberjacks, climbing out of their quick foxholes,
Inched toward the fight for a look at what was what.
The mountain was zero, it was a hill of pebbles,
And out of its powder, with the black-and-blue loser
By the arm, and his shirt in rags, walked the winner
By a knockout, the Yankee wonder, the rose of Dixie,
And the world superheavyweight champ, Paul Bunyan.
He tugged Big Swede on back to the ramshackle camp,
And old Paul rubbed his red knuckles, and said real slow,
'I'm sorry; you're a horse, and I should have backed you.
Won't you be my straw boss? I love the way you hit!'
Big Swede, his eyes blue fight, said okay with a laugh,
And after shaking on it, he shouted up a work gang.
The bout was over, but all the blood had knotted on
What was now the great prairie, and the cakes of dirt
Balled up with blood were the Black Hills of Dakota.

3

They saw the mountains go boom in the awful shock wave
From the big fight between Paul Bunyan and Big Swede,
And the lumberjack shanties shake till they were timber,
And looking through the sticks and damage, old Paul yelped:
The ink barrels in his head office had split their ribs
And spilled ink all over his day journals and log books;
The tallies were splashed, and the characters were smeared,
The rigmarole was illegible, everything was blackened
Up to volume ten thousand, the stories said the end,
Oh the flashy and the old-fashioned words were lost,
And he winced, and laid his raw palm against his cheek:
'God, why do I have to rip through this flimsy camp
Like a pig at a wedding? While I brawl and I feather
My cap I catastrophe what I love; I'm all the mayhem
I need, I banged up these shanties, these innocent books
With my own fist! Look: my bouncing chronicles are spoiled,
The long gambles and the grand slams are wiped out now,
And I don't care how many god-damn dollars I pile up
Or prayers I squawk to the sky, I can't buy them back.
Okay, the boys and I are in a pinch, it's time to light
Into a whiz-bang and history-making job, and quick;
Oh my crazy lumberjacks, if I know you from nothing
A wrangle, yeah! you cocks, a double drive is just
What'll set your boots on fire, and boost you to the clouds!'
Old Paul and his mob shoved off, looking for a creek
For the double drive: they skipped Powder River, since
It's so wide and so shallow, till where it rolls over
And it's so skinny and so deep, and they laughed off
Salt River, all snags and velocity, and kept on walking;
They snorted at the white water boiling in the Hot Springs,
And while it's true it promised all kinds of good logging,
Nobody wanted to go up Shit Creek, because the idea
Sounded funny; they pushed on to the east anyhow,
Till somewhere out in the Wisconsin sticks they hit
The Side-by-Side Rivers, the water cresting, and slick
As a swindle; it looked perfect, but after scouting it
Out they saw the hitch: while the rivers were dandy,
The timber was skimpy by the shoreline, oh maybe
A winter's firewood and that's it, and old Paul sat
In his new office, sketching, working on an angle.
He was still stymied a couple of pots of coffee later,

When, popping his knuckles, he sauntered to the window
And sprawled back: it was hard to swallow, but he saw
What looked like a pine forest out there, out of nowhere,
With a chance of trees, and all of them big and bare,
Buckskin and topless, like a logger's kingdom come,
It was better than a kick in the head by a blue ox!
It was kind of spooky with the freak pines standing
In rows, but it's how come they'd be fine without trail
Swamping, it was a lightning show: the boys were drooling,
And when old Paul looked up from the amazing orchard,
He only sneezed, and pow! they jumped in, swinging axes!
He was real tickled to see his brush monkeys wheel
And the question mark answer itself, and he dilly-
Dallied awhile on the way back to his pencil shoving.
Highballing like fire through the amazing orchard,
Shearing the trees into big blue butts, the timber beasts,
Appleknockers, animals and punks, floaters and palookas,
Broke into the green timber: the double drive was led
On the left Side-by-Side by the bull moose, Big Swede,
On the right by the ramrod, Soupbone Tom, log-hungry
And money-mad, who was so skinny he had to stand
In the sun ten lousy minutes to throw a shadow,
And wore a double-barrel shotgun for a pair of pants.
It was a race, there were troublemakers screwing up,
And the bull bucks name-calling to crack down on them:
On the sheepherders, who couldn't hit a bull in the ass
With a shovel, and the grape grabbers, on the lookout
For the short haul, the bible pounders, with their nerve
And their noise, on the punks and whittlers, who whipped
All morning without any muscle, and the sightseers
And witnesses, out gawking instead of pitching in, and
On the buckwheaters, who were all thumbs, hopeless, slow
As grandmas, and didn't know a broadax from a banjo.
Now most of the men were lightfoot gut-busting horses,
All iron and steam, out to be on the blue ribbon side,
Working the back country, and skipping anything less
Than six feet wide, tackling the barber poles, crooked
As ram's horns, hollow trees, redtops dying of beetles,
Wolf trees, on a perhaps, fat pines and bastard firs,
Rampikes, blowdowns, and the clear long-bodied saw timber,
And falling the ice-broken bayonet tops, stagheads, cripples,

Timber with stubs, burls, swells, crowfeet, spike knots,
Scars, and pitch pockets, out in the windshake woods.
After the swampers had brushed out the walking trails,
A logger, singlejacking by himself, fixing to fall a pine,
Would shoo off the yellow jackets and the mean horseflies,
Keep his eye out for a hidebehind, the man-eater, always
In back of him, bite off a chaw of fancy dynamite
Eating tobacco, grab hold of his ax by the blister end,
Whistle something while planting his bergman calked shoes
In the tiger crap, lift up his ax, swing solid, whack out
An undercut, dodge splinters spit by the argopelters,
Corner her up, shuffle around, chop the back cut out,
And sing out, Down the hill! as the pole croaked and fell,
Smashing on over like slapstick, and busting its crown.
Now's when the beavers got eager, knocking off the limbs
And the knots with boy's axes, getting their misery harps,
Their crosscut saws, oiling them up with cougar juice,
And sawing hell for speed, if they got timber-bound,
They'd widen the cut with wedges, bucking all the trees
To logs, kicking up sawdust. Now the bullwhackers came
To bunch up the pay poles, bridle them round with rope
And pull, straining their milk, drag them to the skid road,
Where the blue ox was hauling for both of the teams,
Snaking logs to the two rivers, where the canthook men
Rolled and decked them on the rollways, ready to drive,
With Big Swede and Soupbone Tom stacked up in a tie.
With the fat cut booming out of the bush, the bookkeeping
Was doubled, and old Paul just blinked, as mixed up
As a handful of ants, trying to count up the infinite
On his fingers. Once he looked up from his book juggling
And it struck him that the left twin was six feet high
And rising, while the right was okay, and so, puzzling
Why the river was all jacked up, and anxious about
The rollways, he went downstream to take a gander.
He saw what he thought was a rumptifusel, wrapped
Round a tree trunk like a fur coat, and pure vicious,
And jogging on, he tried to track a toteroad shagamaw,
Walking on its front bear claws, on its back moose hoofs,
And sniffing for lumberjack clothes hanging on the pines.
When he was a country mile down, he bumped into it:
There was a work boot out in the belly of the river

And backing the water, which was worn by a man taller
Than the mortal law, sitting up on this bluff, and when
He jiggled his foot out of the branch, the flood let go.
Old Paul eyeballed this stranger, pretty near as big as him,
Baldheaded, with a high forehead full of logic wrinkles,
And with sky-pale blue eyes behind his golden spectacles,
Which perched on his long snout, and who bit on his lips
And fiddled with his necktie, as he scraped a jackknife
Big as a bull across a limestone cliff, making it flat
And throwing off flakes like snow; up from behind his ear
He snatched the original lead pencil, made of a coon tree,
And scribbled on the bluff, making numbers, up and down,
And all oblivious to Paul Bunyan, which is no breeze.
Paul waved his burly arms, and he hopped like a pigeon;
He uprooted a fir, but nothing doing, and so he drawled,
'Yeah, it sure's going to be dry if it don't ever rain.'
The stranger didn't flinch, he just kept on writing
And so Paul plumped down beside him on the cliff and said,
'Pardon me if I say howdy; it's a mighty morning.
I think I'll just help myself to a chaw of this here
Peerless spit-or-puke tobacco: you're welcome to it
If you like, it tastes ferocious. Well, how's it going?'
The stranger looked up, real casual, and he sighed, 'Oh,
I'm just staggering around: I don't know, I feel funny,
My hair's flying off in clumps, my eyes are shot to heck,
I've got chapped lips, my teeth all hurt, my breath is awful,
I've got a bellyache, cramps in what I call my muscles,
My ass is sore from the applejack sprints, I'm horny
And my cock's out of whack, oh my knees are buckling,
My dogs are woofing and I'm scared to count the blisters,
Insects are ganging up on me and eating me alive,
I think I'm having a sunstroke, what are the symptoms,
I'm sick, my wind's broken, my heart's running by prayer,
Oh I'm in great shape, pal, I'll be okay if I live.
I believe I will indulge myself with a twist of scrap;
Why hell, you know since all of you hillbillies are hooked
On chewing tobacco, I ought to market an out west brand;
Ads, billboards, sandwich boys, listen to the campaign:
Dazzle the boss, and wow all the gals with just one nip
Of this champion funky all-American plug tobacco!
I'd have to scalp it, you see, knock it down dirt-cheap

To cut under the boys back east; I could branch out
And pocket a cool million, oh and I mean clean up!
It sure beats melting in these god-forsaken boondocks.'
Old Paul was thinking this bird swallowed a dictionary,
And he was doing his level best to keep from grinning:
'You won't be hot long, stranger, buck up: it looks like rain.'
'Are you kidding? Have you sized up the old firmament,
Or what? Why, these cat's-tail clouds are all hocus-pocus.
I want to wise you up, big boy: clouds are supposed
To be the great chiefs of the wild blue, right? Like hell;
I say they can't organize a piss in a beer parlor!
Oh yeah, they bluster, but don't let that bamboozle you;
They're all thunder and no rain, trust me; underneath,
When it comes to sky juice, they're a bunch of pinch fists.'
'I wish I had a notion of what the heck you're talking
About, but don't say: I'd like to hear what you're writing.'
'I'm working on this plus this, that take away that,
So-and-so times whatever, and nothing into something;
In a word, I'm figuring: I guess it's like a hobby.'
Old Paul slipped off the cliff, dusted off and then yelled,
'Hold on! Gracious me, you do arithmetic for fun?'
'Oh natch, corn cracker, I'm so hot for numbers, ha!
I love it: all the honky-tonks out here in gay Wisconsin,
And I work! I can't fandango in the middle of nowhere!'
The man's an artist, thought Bunyan, he works for nothing!
'Howdy! I'm Paul Bunyan, tramp, big shot, tall talker,
Trail swamper, ax swinger, pine tree bucker, log driver,
Pioneer, lightning thinker, and all-round superlumberjack.'
'Hi ya, Mister Bunyan. I'm John Rodgers Inkslinger,
Answer man, math whiz, ballyhoo man, land surveyor,
Country doctor, local comic, and back street philosopher.
I'm actually working on a rough geography problem.'
'Well, break it to me, Johnny: I've done some figuring
And I know the layout here; maybe I can help you.'
'Okay, here goes: I'm looking for section thirty-seven.
In surveyor's measure, there's thirty-seven square miles
In a township, but out here I only count thirty-six;
I walk it over, thirty-six; I add it up backwards,
Thirty-six! What happened? I ain't fooling, it's a pain
In the atlas: if I didn't blow it, surveying is bunk!'
'Now hold everything. When I logged off the lower Side-

By-Side Rivers, I'd hitch Babe, my blue ox, to a section,
On account of old Babe can haul anything with two ends,
Tow it to the river, cut down the good and plenty timber,
And drag the square of land back to its original spot.
I always let the thirty-seventh sit in the water
While I went on a coffee break, and it'd wash away.
I guess you better switch to a scale of thirty-six.'
Inkslinger squinted with surprise, and started jabbering,
'Well, I'll be hornswoggled! You'd make a hot surveyor;
Why you're no country egg, or frontier rowdy! Look,
Why don't you hook up with me and be a mud chicken?
With your latitude and my longitude, there's no limit;
We could pace off this continent down to the last pebble,
And I promise the work'll go down like morning wildfire!
Don't be shy, muscle man: what is it, yep or nope?'
'I've got a big idea under my hunting cap, Johnny,
Which I'm hoping will come out in front of the parade:
Why don't you sign on with me and be a timekeeper?
You'd be the brains and count the stacks of timber for me,
Reckon up the payroll and dream up theories for laughs,
Crank out your heart's journal, and in your own words,
Witness our lumberjacking and write it down, guts, feathers
And all, oh glory, Inkslinger, you were born for the job!
The pay is slim, but man! the exaltation's evergreen.
Why don't you take a whirl at it, and see what's up?'
'No thanks, you keep your rough-hustling lumber camp,
I'll stick to my compass and chain: I've come this far,
I want to go the distance, I want to map America.
Hey, will you ask your blue ox to quit licking my cheek?
I mean, I love animals, but enough is enough, huh?
Oh, no! What's this? What in the hell is this? Oh shit!
Your dumb stinking ox trampled on my instruments!
My charts, my scopes, my pencils, my lines, my tables,
My cheating sticks, they're all stomped on by the blue beast,
It's all over! Ah, I might as well just kiss it off!'
'Hang on, Johnny. I apologize for the blue ox, honest,
But don't you act like a nincompoop and start bawling!
Okay, two-fisted calamity's knocked you for a loop:
What do you do, caterwaul like a kid, or bang back
Like a cowboy? I say why dive, on a random punch?
I all but wiped out my tall chronicles in a fight,

But damn if I was whipped: I just spit and jolted on.
Now, don't boohoo: come on, let's tromp over to the camp.
No sweat, you'll get your share of sun circles, like when
The boys and I struck out, after the above skirmish,
And walked as big as anything into this amazing orchard
Where all we had to do was yank out the pines like that!
I'm spouting off, I just wish you wouldn't say it's over;
Nothing this side of sunlight can lick a lumberjack.
Look, over yonder's where the nothing-to-it timber stood.'
Inkslinger pointed, with his skimpy hair pricking up like
Wild bristles on an old broom, and he stood and squawked,
'Oh, nausea! I don't believe it! Oh lord! Help, police!
All of my surveyor's stakes! They're all gone, you crook!
Go get them, you bastard: you better haul them back!'
'I'm sure they're sawed up by now; I'm sorry, I didn't know.'
'Oh great! Goodbye two years of real baldheaded work!
I rooted them deep, man: those poles were going to weather!
Hey, I feel lousy. Everything looks yellow; my skin is numb!'
Inkslinger spluttered, stretched out his arms, wobbled
And said oh-oh like a moo cow, doubled up like a sack
Of Idaho potatoes, and slumped into a mud puddle.
Old Paul leaned down and lugged him fireman style into
The back room of his shanty, where he let him snooze;
And the low surveyor took to roosting in that tight room,
Kind of sulky and nothing to say. The drive poked along
Till the blues hit old Paul, and he thumped on the door:
'Johnny, it's Bunyan. I swear, I feel dumb as a man
With a size seventeen collar and a size two hat for,
You know, my stake mistake, and when the ox ran loose
All over your gear. If I had two heads, I'd let you
Knock them together. I guess I am a country egg,
I should have known; boy, it's so hard to build whatever,
And so easy to bust it up. I owe you, Inkslinger.
I could kick myself, but that's silly. I could trap you,
Oh, say a gyascutus: it's big as a buck in winter,
And with blue lightning in its eyes, jack rabbit ears,
Mountain lion jaws, and a yowl like a southeast blow,
It's no wonder you can't see it till after a snake bite,
Sloping across the foothills, up on its telescope legs,
Hanging on tight with its rainbow tail, and eating rocks.
If your pleasure's fire water, I can bring you a fat jug

Of my wild juniper moonshine: it's righteous, cutthroat,
And with beer back, look out! It's a true antifogmatic,
It'll whoopee you up in no time, as sure as preaching.
Would you go for the complete works of Bigmouth Bill,
In forty volumes, with woodcuts, a forward, backward,
Index, glossary, concordance, gazetteer, and almanac?'
Paul stopped and rubbed his chin, and Inkslinger sneered,
'The more you stir it, the more it stinks. Give it up.'
After this slam old Paul was so stung in his heart
He let his chronicles go and lost track of the logging,
And though the Side-by-Side drive was a four-star hit,
He only sat there, calculating how to make it up
To Johnny, when the surveyor shuffled out and said,
'Okay, Mister Big, fetch your books: I'm signing on.'
Paul went straight up at this, and hollered from the clouds,
'What on earth! Are you fooling me, Johnny? What happened?'
'I'm coming to it, blue eyes: with all this ripe time,
I figured I might thumb through your old chronicles.
Now, when I'm in bad shape, I'm a sucker for myself,
But while I read, I stopped thinking about my sour luck:
Why, you're an ax-slinging wonder, you son of a bitch!'
'How'd you read the chronicles? They're covered with ink!'
'Wait just a second here, and I'll let you have a look.'
Johnny came back out with book one of the chronicles:
He'd traced over the goose feather scratches in the paper
In white ink, religiously, bringing back the alphabet,
And he'd salvaged all of the ten thousand volumes.
Old Paul stared, and he said with a catch in his voice,
'I'm proud to know you, Johnny; but why'd you do all this?'
'I'm in love with you, high pockets, what do you think?
No, really: sulking gets to be duller than Wisconsin
After a while, and patching up the chronicles was fun.'
'Oh Johnny Inkslinger, you're in! Shake hands, partner.'

4

Paul Bunyan roused and back-slapped his solid work gang,
Big Swede barked out the show like a circus ringmaster,
Johnny Inkslinger spelled it all out in the big book,
And the camp trekked to Saginaw country, Michigan.
Out on the grizzly and snow-stacked Tittabawasee
They split timber and piled the rollways up to the sky,
Old Paul now logging elbow to elbow with his boys.
Yeah, but spring staggered in with an air of trouble:
Come April, the boys were standing out on the old Manistee,
And when the ice shivered the tail down men broke rollways,
Jabbing their canthooks, shoving the saw logs in the river,
And the water rats followed, tramping down gig trails
Along the frosty shore, and riding on rafts and booms,
Kicking out the jams, tangling with the skookumchuck:
Waterfalls, whirlpools, narrows, tiderips, neverstills.
The slough pigs at the tail end of the misty parade,
Whirling swingdogs, yawping, laid back, sacking the rear,
Rolling the draggers and strays in the almighty water,
And nobody but was two hoots from a timber wolf.
All of a sudden, without a howdy-do, scads of mosquitoes
With sixteen-foot wingspreads dove down out of nowhere,
Straddled the creek, and started shanghaiing lumberjacks!
One old strong-arm logger fought free of the varmints
And slooped straight out of the blue, falling so far
The dang bluebirds built a nest on his windy head
And hatched their daughters and sons before he hit home.
Old Paul saw the whole gallinipper sneak attack,
And he shuttled Brimstone Bill the bullwhacker south
On a hot pony and at full pay for the Pecos River
To round up fighting Texas bumblebees, big and pronto.
Bill rode across the Oklahoma flats so all-honking fast
He saw the gosh-darn wind: he riled the hives up good,
Was a star in a whip-crack rodeo, and drove the swarm
Back from Texas to Michigan without losing a bee.
The ugly pushflies, with their hot heads and ring tails,
Slammed into the mosquitoes under a scab-red sun,
Whacking their wings like wet buzzards, and squirting fire;
But after a dogfight, the insect mobs fixed it up
And went in cahoots, cranking out a bunch of crossbreeds:
The moskittos, with stingers at both the front and back,
And just a monstropolous fancy for hooktenders' oxen.

They were death on ox snatching: they'd corner an ox
In the corral, fly up to it with a sling of leather
And buzz under, spin a bowknot, tighten the loop,
And good night Irene. Old Paul had holed up his herd
In a skeeter-proof cave, when the moskittos roared back
And hit that rock whining, working down like steam drills,
Dropping a shaft to the ox cave, shooting up lightning.
The moskittos were two rods deep in north country rock
When the loggers saw them jam up against a quartz vein,
And hold up to point their stingers: the nearest sandstone
Was clear in Minnesota, and so Paul had time to tick.
He dragged out an old kitchen boiler, stuck an ox in it,
Scrunched on in with Big Ole the blacksmith, and grinned.
The moskittos swooped up and got a whiff of the ox,
Whizzed a spell in the air, and zoomed in on a beeline:
As soon as a stinger drilled through, old Paul and Big Ole
Banged it over with their ten-pound sledges like carpenters
Clinching nails, till the whole mob was hooked to the iron.
The boiler rocked and rose as the ox rustlers took off,
And quick Paul and the blacksmith jumped Geronimo,
With the ox in their arms: the moskittos flapped away,
And were never seen again, especially by greenhorns.
To loosen up and just dawdle after the carryings-on,
Old Paul shouldered his pine-butt straight-barrel flintlock
And hiked on out to hunt in the freezing Michigan woods.
Just a spit and a holler out of camp, he got a flash
Of an actual gumberoo, looking for burned-out woods,
With a pumpkin head and a potbelly like a stove,
Ape arms and crazy legs sticking out round its waist;
It'd heave itself off a slope and roll down sideways,
Squeaking like a pulley, and scared of nothing but fire,
Because if it ever rubbed up against a flame, kerblam.
It minded him of when he sighted a whirling whimpus,
Which was a scraggly bastard, as big as a rain barrel,
With its plow horse legs all grown together at the fetlock
Into one hoof, and skinny arms which were so long
It steadied itself by propping on its palms. If a man
Was dumb enough to sidle up next to a whimpus,
It would cakewalk and whirligig like a wino on ice:
A crack from the whirling fists would cream the guy,
And the whirling whimpus would lick him up like pudding.

He thought of his staring contest with a flock of huggags,
Which stood thirteen feet high and weighed in at three tons,
With mud balls instead of heads and warts on their snouts,
Gunny sacks for ears, pine needle coats, and big flat feet.
The huggags go grazing in herds, on pitch and sweat,
And when it's time for shut-eye, since they have no knees
And can't flop down, the herd faces northwest by the moon
And sags against the trees, which, under three-ton pressure,
Begin to slant after a couple of nights; in American woods,
A stretch of timber all tilting one way is a sure sign
Huggags have been sleeping there. Just for the heck of it,
Bunyan figured out how to go about catching a huggag:
It'd be simple to pick out one of these skew-jaw trees
And saw it halfway; the idea's when a huggag went
To lean back for the old siesta, the trunk would rip
And the huggag go down, and, without knees, stay down.
Now Paul wasn't out for lop-eared gazooks and such like,
And so he aimed his heart and gun sight at a flight
Of two hundred twelve wild ducks skidding in pattern:
But why blow a slug on each and every nothing duck
In the sky? It was just plain wasteful, period. So
He tied a ball of twine to a bullet, loaded his rifle
And yawned, and when the ducks were lined up, he fired,
The twine went flying, the bullet harpooned all two-twelve,
And he tugged them back to camp like trout on a thread.
On his second outing, he went on the prowl for partridge,
And arguing like before that one shot ought to be plenty.
At last he spotted three hundred and twenty partridges
All pluming and twittering on a white spruce bough,
And he crouched, sighting longwise down the pretty branch,
Waiting for a bear to come bumbling and puffing along,
And when a big black bear wobbled up, old Paul squeezed:
The bullet went sparkling through the bear, split the limb,
The partridges' feet dropped down in the sudden crack,
The crack sprung shut, pinching all the birds to the bough,
Which broke off with a bang, tumbled in the air, and clouted
A burly deer in back of a juniper bush, wild honey
Poured out of the rip in the spruce, the deer kicked and
Slugged a fat buck rabbit up smack into Paul's forehead,
Paul teetered and flopped in the creek, and wading out
With his pockets full of fish, he headed back to camp,

Bringing, in his haul with a single bullet, a black bear,
Three hundred and twenty partridges, a buck rabbit,
A good-looking eight-point deer, a passel of catfish,
And two rolling hundred gallon barrels of wild honey.
On his third tramp, Bunyan was loaded for Red Eye,
The ugly bull moose who was tall as Suicide Hill,
With famous eyes like railroad lanterns, and great horns.
He brought a bullet and an ox wagon full of popcorn,
Which was his favorite snack when it was salty and buttered,
And deep in a pole thicket, a couple of rattlesnakes,
Coiling, clicking, flickered out at his boot: he sneered
And, twiddling his whiskers, hitched their heads together,
And, inch by inch, the sidewinders swallowed each other
Down to the rattles, and disappeared like abracadabra.
On a high cliff yonder, Red Eye was munching the grass,
As fat as a December bear, and bored with hunters:
The trick was how to blow it down without knocking
The moose, which was nobody's fool, off of the cliff;
And so old Paul sniffed and combobbolated a moment,
And when an idea lit up like morning in his attic
He nodded, diving into the popcorn for energy, chewing
With a clatter as loud as a Kentucky free-for-all,
And whisking it in so fast his hands were all blurry;
The wind off his fingers jerked trees out by the roots,
And the country acres around was drifted a foot deep
In popcorn scraps, and all the quill pigs and swish tails,
When they saw the ground white and the sky full of flakes,
Figured they were out in a snowstorm, and froze.
With his smoke pole reared, the butt cradled in his shoulder,
Old Paul grunted, 'I aim to let fly and massacre you
Between the eyes: now get ready for circumbustification;'
He drew a bead, laid off breathing, and let her blaze,
And he lit out lickety-split for the moose, skedaddling
Quick as a boy and girl get naked under a honeymoon,
Hustling up there to grab old Red Rye before he fell,
So breath-taking fast he'd just touch a foot down now
And again to steer, red-faced like he was stealing home
On a wild ball, in a level game, in the last inning,
Two away, with a full count on a cross-eyed rookie;
But it was crazy, he ran just a suspicion too fast
And showed up at the moose before his own damn bullet.

He was chortling at this when it was time to duck,
As the shot went zinging over his hat, and it missed
Between the antlers, but Red Eye was already stiff:
The varmint had recognized old Paul and died of shock.
While he was slogging the miles home, with a new smile,
Paul Bunyan made chin music to keep him company:
'Bunch up the Dixie swamps and the Bible belt prairies,
The holy down East farms and the wild West beaches,
Throw in the cities with their shows and skidrow queens,
And all the screamers in this checkerboard of states,
Wrap them in Great Plain clouds and tie it with Old Muddy,
And like a dime firecracker next to the Milky Way,
Where the Fourth of July will spin till half past always,
The whole shebang is beat out by the Northern woods.
Now that the snow's thawing and jazzing up the creeks
And the midmorning moon's a white wreck in the sky,
The springs boom and improvise the reedy sloughs, and
Wake up the lakes, whose style is to double in water
Three seasons of the tough poles in the swank forest.
The long grasses hang on and mob out of the mud
Under the green snarl of wild holly and huckleberry,
And up with the looting bluejays and whiskey jacks,
In the tight bark whose calligraphy nobody can read,
The old evergreen timber muscles toward the light.
I hike the Northern woods with a kick in my sally,
I soak up the world like it was highballing away,
And once I snort the backwoods air into my pipes
My eyes ignite and my toes curl, I cock my elbows
Because I'm so slap-happy, and I arch my back and yowl
Like a lean coyote with all the stars in his head!
The animals may be a touch on the rampageous side,
But I can manhandle anything with bones, yeah
I can buck-dance with a wildcat and laugh him down,
I can snuff a timber wolf with a couple of blue words:
I'll wrestle Mrs. Nature three falls out of three
And stake my ox and all that I come up immortal,
And still steamed up with love for the curve of the earth.
I declare! Fire, infection and Yankees only slow her up,
And she's handsome as a keg of beer in a heat wave.
The pitch climbs in the pines, and my sap jumps in me
I feel so gully-whumping good when I look out

On a Northern morning and see the pine cones bulge
On the branches, and the daylight lean against the trees.'
When Paul got back to his choppers he was full of bang
And the logging was too slow-motion to please his pulse,
And he whistled like he was mad, and staggered them up:
'What kind of a one-dollar chicken-shit outfit is this,
You jerkwater slow-poke wishy-washy deadhead
Flat-beer pussyfooting lollygagging drag-ass punks!
I turn my back to spit and whiz, and you guys peter out!
I'm sorry to crack up your gingerbread dreams, ladies,
But when I said to saw logs I didn't mean snore!
You bunch of whittlers are useful as a one-legged man
At a kicking match! I want to see Swedish steam
Spout out of your temples; get dirty, give her snoose!
I catch a man boondoggling and I'll eat him for lunch!
Wade in and knock it down, show the jungle you're alive!'
Paul picked out the top loggers in the Saginaw camp,
Red Jack, Rocky Dan, Pumphandle Joe, Slabwood Johnson,
Billy the Bum, Cedar Root Charley, and Roaring Jim,
Called them the seven axmen, swapped their ax handles
For iron chains, and let them swing their double-bit heads
Like sodbusters in August out mowing the south forty.
It was still too slow, so Paul invented the two-man saw
And worked it with Big Swede: its blade was around a mile,
And it swiped an acre at a whack. In the rough country
It skimmed hills and ridges, it skipped gorges and flumes,
But the two champions bulldozed whole counties anyhow.
While they were hitching up the load to Babe the blue ox,
The clouds curdled and dumped down a goose-drowning rain,
And when Babe, strong as a bullwhacker, pulled homeward,
The wet leather harness, under the strain of tons,
Stretched out like gossip on the general store porch.
When they rolled into camp, Paul discovered the harness
Running clear out to the skyline and the load beyond,
And he wheezed and chuckled till the sun came out,
The buckskin shriveled, and the lumber chugged to his feet.
The rain water had spilled so awful hard in the downpour
The rain barrel, which held nine hundred eighty-nine barrels,
Twenty-eight gallons, one quart, one-half pint, one gill
And three tablespoons minus eight drops, filled thirteen feet
And ten inches over the top, old Houghton Lake overflowed

And the Muskegon River ran too fast to sip from it:
The boys were scared the current might rip off their heads.
Old Paul rounded up the river rats and the boom pokes
And started the drive, yelling tips from the book of snags;
But as soon as the wood was wet they hit a log jam,
With a big pole stuck and a whole stack-up behind it,
And if a monkey were to shin up the jackpot to free it,
He'd be sure to be crunched before he could say scat.
Now, planting the blue ox down-river in front of the jam,
Old Paul fired off his shotgun, aiming to tickle Babe's ass
With buckshot till his tail twirled like a screw in the water,
Which washed it backwards, and untangled the rack heap.
Bunyan and his river hogs, with their peaveys in their fists,
Steadied out on the timber, and barreled down the flood
On the backs of the logs, heading for a far-off sawmill.
After sailing for a spell, Paul called to Roaring Jim,
'Hey, check out the lumber camp on your southpaw bank!
I could have sworn we were lonesome in Michigan, Jim:
You ever catch word of a logging gang up against us?'
Roaring Jim squinted at the pine shanties and said,
'No, man: I ain't heard a hoot about any competition,
But it sure as eggs looks like we've bumped into it!
It's too bad, but we're floating by too fast to ask them.'
Old Paul yanked his slouch hat down to his boiling ears
And took a bite of his squirting tobacco, spiked his log
And snarled at the white water as they all coasted by
The tingling spruce groves, on the lookout for boulders.
When they burbled round a long crescent in the river
Paul stiffened up like a scarecrow in a frost and shouted,
'Okay, Roaring Jim! I'm about to go nuts: why don't
You cock your eyes to the left, and sing out what you see.'
Roaring Jim rubbed his eyes, stooped down and looked out:
'Say I'm all wet, but it's another camp! Yeah, this one
Is slightly bigger; but hold on to your petticoats,
Am I slipping, or is that camp kind of familiar?'
Old Paul sneezed and answered, 'I don't know, Roaring Jim;
All I know's this country's getting a trace too crowded,
I see another lumber camp, I'm going to get curious!'
He leaned out, looking alive: it gave him butterflies
In his stomach and a shooting star in his idea box, but
He just drove on through the haze, boosting up his boys,

Tending out, and sticking to his skill and his hunches.
The singsong water was making him drowsy and timeless,
As he rode on its skin, and rippled around a slow curve,
When he jolted and stared at a big money lumber camp
On his left hand, and he hollered, 'All right, damn it:
All hands and the cook and the woodpeckers, ashore!'
The river rats steered over to the bank, and Bunyan said,
'Ain't this a beauty? We're back at our camp. If you boys
Imagine we're going ahead, you've been stung by creation.
Oh we're not too swift this morning! We're on a round river.
We can paddle from now to Christmas, we're going nowhere,
And it'll be the same hawk, blackberry bush and lumber camp
In the Great Lakes country sun after ten thousand years.
This creek has no spring and no bay: it's circled back
And turned us into tourists, I swear to Yankee Doodle!'
Paul was about to take a tall shovel and cut a canal
Slapdash to the lake from the make-believe backwater,
But he saw that the Round River was a wonder-for-hogs,
And so, hauling the timber overland to the Muskegon,
Old Paul launched the whole lollapaloozing drive again!
He was so star-spangled exultant at the big finish
He celebrated the fact by dreaming up water walking:
He broad-jumped way out to a long log in mid-river
And rolled it with his stride till the water creamed;
He stomped like a turkey, and while he birled he bragged:
'Whoopee! I'm long-legged, I'm rambunctious, I'm ripe!
I'm all bouncy, I'm the spotted horse nobody can ride!
Yeah, I waddle like an ox and I crow like a cyclone,
I punch like a landslide and I fuck like a hummingbird!
I'd walk ten miles in a good hurricane for a fight!
I've got the guts of a god-almighty freight train
And the brains of an almanac! Oh, I'm an easy hobo;
I can take a bite out of the sun and spit light,
I can strut till a buffalo blushes, and outscream you!
Look out, boys, I'm freewheeling and I'm on the loose!'
And he hoofed it so strong that when the river rumpled
He walked ashore on the bubbles, cut a gig trail,
And skipped back to the log before the bubbles broke.

5

When they had wound up the haywire Round River show,
The sawdust eaters decided on a drift to the west,
Out towards Red River and the hard Minnesota winter
In the country of bread and butter and the North Star,
Globe-trotting on the tail of the floater, Paul Bunyan.
The pot wrestler, known to the boys as the belly robber,
Was named Pea Soup Shorty, and was so dead-in-the-bone
And let-it-slide lazy, he'd railroaded his flunkies
Into sniffing the green slop in the kettle for him
Because, he said, it tuckered him out to breathe that deep.
He ruled out groceries one by one: first, porcupine stew,
And then slumgullion, bubble and squeak, and mystery pie,
Till he'd cut all the meals back to nothing but pea soup,
Pea soup today and forever, with a taste like fog.
He froze it around ropes and shipped it out as sticks,
He got the idea of sloshing it into the hollow ax handles
So the swinging of the axes would keep the soup hot,
And when Shagline Bill's freight sleds cracked up on the ice
And spilled into a lake, Pea Soup Shorty strolled out there
With a half a hog and three crates of Arkansas chicken,
Which is long for salt pork, dumped it in with black pepper,
Bloomed up a fire under the lake and made pea soup.
When he was running low, he sliced each pea in two
And boiled up a barrel of the world's first split pea soup;
And when they gave out, the bum salted a green shirt
And dunked it in the kettle, and nobody noticed. After
That, Brimstone Bill the bullwhacker walked up to Paul
To squawk for the boys, and blared till he was blue:
'Oh, for crying out loud in the clatterwhacking morning!
I'll be shot for a mockingbird before I touch a drop
Of this god-awful slime, and that goes for my pals!
I'd rather eat wind sandwiches, or a stack of knotholes!
This sad flat pie-face you hired on as a stew builder
Won't build a stew, on account of he's too busy looking
To slow-poison us all with pea soup, I ain't humming!
I've had my gutful of the bastard: he's a washout
As a soup jockey; he could be replaced by a fart!
I see a splash of soup and I'll puke up my breakfast!
Hey, you know I don't bellyache, I'm too straight-grained,
And it's got to be the limit when I get the gripes!
Come on, give the runt the ax, before we all keel over!'

Bunyan was too red-blooded to let his men fly off
Over bad chow, and he sacked Pea Soup Shorty that minute,
And boosted Sourdough Sam, who had been the crumb boss,
Up to grease burner: he was no slouch, but a high-stepping
Old horse, and sort of a crackpot about his one subject,
Sourdough, and not from buck fever like Pea Soup Shorty,
Who started in to pushing pea soup out of pure laziness;
Sam took a forty-two caliber devotion to sourdough
In the way that a gospel pitcher loves Jerusalem Slim.
Sam was daffy about sourdough, and he moved from biscuits
To sourdough salad, sourdough hamburgers, sourdough coffee,
And now he dreamed of a seven-course all-sourdough spread.
Sourdough rises upwards of five times as fast as yeast
And it's dynamite to handle, which didn't hold Sam back
From bragging it to the moon like a salesman, and claiming
It worked as pillow feathers, candle wax and gun powder,
And when swallowed as a pill, it would cure all miseries
From hay fever and black eyes to boils and summer colds.
Now a crab, a stranger by the name of Blowhard Ike,
Had blown into the camp, spare, toplofty, and peaked,
With this eye squinting and that one looking up for rain,
A man who pranced an inch too high for a raw hand.
He showed up in front of Johnny Inkslinger and spat,
'Hey! I'm the new swamper, and I'm here to draw my gear.'
Inkslinger wagged his pen and spoke up in a flat voice,
'Hang on, you long-tailed barnstorming son of a whore,
I'm sweating out a brain tickler in high algebra:
I'm looking for the fourth proportional to three vectors
In a common plane,' 'Give me a break, four-eyes: will you
Cut out the crap? Give me my stuff, and I'll toddle off.'
Inkslinger tilted back, peering over his goggles, and said,
'Okay, speedball. Okay now, hold out your rosy hands,
And here's your freaks: your cork boots, turkey for plunder
And such, two face, toe splitter, muck stick, bung starter,
Bear cat, and Swede fiddle: all right, you're a run cutter.'
Blowhard Ike stooped a little under the tools and lingo,
And sidled out the door while Johnny covered up a smile.
Ike swung clattering up to the saw boss with a snarl,
'Show me the swampers, sir: I pretty well know the ropes.'
'Hot dog! Let's shake our hands! Howdy-do, Mister Blowhard?
Yoohoo! Hey boys, stump on over here! It's the green horn.

Boys, meet Mister Blowhard, meet the boys, I'm Big Swede!
I see you've got your diddlewhacky and your thingumajigs,
I guess you're all set. Come on! Oh, and bring your whatsit.'
Ike stood in the grinning ring, with no idea which tool
Was the whatsit, and he shouted up at the man mountain,
'What is all this muck fiddle and bear starter nonsense?
How in you know where am I supposed to crack your code?
Why don't you spell it out without all the slang trimmings?'
'Oh shucks, it's easy as strawberries, Mister Blowhard.
First, put your cork boots on. There's your turkey, your pack.
You stick your plunder in there, your letters from mom.
This drag saw's your bear cat, this muck stick's your shovel;
The big ax is a two face, the little ax is a toe splitter;
This thing that looks like a Swede fiddle is your bucksaw,
Oh hold on here! Well, poop! I'm sorry, Mister Blowhard.
You're stuck like a goose. You can't whack the trails today.'
Ike rubbed a red polka dot rag across his brow, and said,
'This camp is beyond me! Why can't I whack the trails?'
'Golly gosh! It's nothing. You're missing your sky hook.
You fetch it from Mister Inkslinger and you'll be fixed.'
Rumbling and snorting across the sea-sloping clearing,
Ike faced the timekeeper on the stoop of his office
And told him about the mix-up and the missing sky hook,
While Johnny nodded, cool as a catbird, and answered,
'My mistake, Ike; I was all coiled up in my graphs
And I clean let it slip; pardon me, and I'll square it.
You just can't be a star swamper without your sky hook,
You old sharpshooting fool; let me haul it out here.'
Inkslinger inched back out, dragging a hulk of a rig
Built out of odd pulleys, crooked augers, big flywheels,
And weighing somewhere in the neighborhood of two tons.
Blowhard Ike was crumbling, but just tightened his jaw
And flexed his horsepower, saying to himself he'd show
These cornball rednecks he wasn't a man to be rattled,
And if they thought he was a lily, he was an iron bull.
He grappled himself all round the infernal contraption
And grunted it into the air: and then, popeyed and snuffing,
And with his cheeks twitching, all of his veins rippling,
And his circle pump thumping for mercy in rag time,
He wobbled sidewise across the cloud-curving field.
It's easy to say iron bull, but his arms were fading out

Just as he came teetering up to the fringe of the sticks,
Red as a whorehouse rug, holding on by his whiskers,
And puffing like a locomotive going up a hog's-back.
Nobody looked at Ike moaning the sky hook down,
They were cocking their ears as Pumphandle Joe talked,
And Ike, wondering what it was all about, listened in:
'I had travelled all the way out there to Yahoo County
To clear up the riddle of the Scarecrow Mine, and sworn
I'd comb the hills from horn to hoof till I struck gold,
By god, and in spite of the three bandits on my tail,
And so I whistled off south and on into Shirttail Bend
Come morning, sleepy, riding my salty lightfooted pinto
Straight through, taking the east fork for Shanghai Hill.
There I could see the cloud kicked up by those cutthroats,
Who could take honey and an anthill and make a man
Give up his daughter, let alone the Scarecrow Mine's secret,
And I wheeled around and struck out for Bluebelly Ravine.
I was aiming to give them the slip by circling back north
And fording a creek a little outside of American Hollow,
Where I hid my pinto and bunked in a squatter's shack,
And he said to go sling the gab with his kin in Ragtown.
Well, by sunup I was three hours on the road east,
Raking my gooseneck spurs and no sign of the outlaws,
And my huddle in Ragtown sent me out to Shinbone Peak,
Far south: the sun sat in the crotch of the two summits,
Just like the old jackass prospector had whispered to me,
And so somewheres hard by here was the lost Scarecrow.
If I'd known the Mine's horror, I'd have bolted the county,
But I rode on from Petticoat Slide to Barefoot Diggings,
Moving westward across the hillsides, rooting for the shaft,
Till I knocked off to camp at dusk, near Brandy Flat.
I guessed the weather looked okay for a star pitch,
I untied my blue bedroll, and saw the bandits' fire.
I was fixing to quit, ah but what the hell, I figured
I had travelled all the way out there to Yahoo County
To clear up the riddle of the Scarecrow Mine, and sworn
I'd comb the hills from horn to hoof till I struck gold,
By god, and in spite of the three bandits on my tail,
And so I whistled off south and on into Shirttail Bend
Come morning, –' Blowhard Ike, all keyed up, interrupted,
'Yeah, but why? Didn't the old prospector say Shinbone Peak?'

The guffaws and the horselaughs came booming down on Ike:
'Haw, haw, haw! The pigeon swallowed it! Shinbone Peak!'
'He was hollering for more! It's just a darling whopper!'
'Oh! He's the dumbest tenderfoot since the Sunday Kid!'
'Hee-haw har-har yuk-yuk ho-ho hee-hee arf-arf!'
Cross-eyed and purple, Ike kicked the machine and barked,
'Yeah, hilarious! Here's the sky hook. Can I get started?'
'Sky hook? Oh no, Ike: that's a smokestack reamer!'
'Dang me if we didn't bamboozle him going and coming!'
'Hey Ike, old scout! Look it up in the swamper's book!'
'Lay off! He can't hardly look it up in that there book,
When it was all eaten up by the tree-dangling hangdowns!'
The mob honked like a flock of mules, as Ike set sail:
What would've just knocked the frills out of a frisky stranger
Sledge-hammered Ike, and he stalked off with a cold eye,
And wound up at the cookshack, bad blood in his veins.
Sourdough Sam was plumping his sourdough rocking chair
Which he'd just slapped together, when Ike stormed in,
All tricked out in his haystack bonnet, his swagger coat,
His flashy new tickle britches, and wet weather shoes,
And, griping like a bulldog, he poured a cup of mud.
Sam stowed his rip chisel in his tool chest and said,
'I want you to be the first in my sourdough rocking chair:
Roll down in the plush, and take it easy: oh, dynamite!'
The rocking chair started in to burbling under Ike,
When it burst open, slobbering all over his deluxe pants:
'Okay, doughface: you can yank out the greenbacks, now!'
'I'm frightful sorry, Ike; I've been fighting a jinx,
Lately: I tell you what, I'll scrub them up just as clean
As a lady with my all-sourdough foam-action soap flakes,
I promise you. Shuck them off, while I mix you up a tub.'
The britches came out of the suds as white as a church,
But Ike whipped them on and cleared out without a word.
The boys kept up the hard riding, nicknaming him Legs,
What with his white pants invisible in the white snow,
And told him he was lucky, he was safe from snow snakes,
Because once he was bit it was tanglefoot oil or death.
Ike hooked every man with, like sniffles or a squeak heel,
And tried to saddle it all on the screw-loose cook
And his lousy sourdough, and he traced athlete's foot,
Whooping cough, baldness, and mosquito bites to sourdough.

After that, the boys would back off from the stink of it,
And work on without their chow, which upset Sourdough Sam;
He was all fussed up like an owl, and talked to Paul,
But the walking boss stood there with winter in his face
And his own worries zinging around his head like blueflies:
It was trying to thaw, and as soon as the ice fractured
Out on Red Lake, the water line would drop perilous low;
If the boys didn't wind it up fast, there'd be no out
To the Red Lake river, with all the lumber landlocked.
Sourdough Sam looked down and poked along to the cookshack,
Where Blowhard Ike sat smoking, and Sam spit and said,
'Ike, I guess it's up the chimney. I might have worked
Natural wonders with my sourdough; and now the boys
Don't even like it as bread. Sourdough's all I can make,
And nobody'll touch it. Ah, there's no snap left in me.'
'Wait, Sam; what about your sourdough ink stretcher?'
Johnny Inkslinger was a skinflint with his ink, since
By rigging up a hose from the ink barrel to his ink stick
And saving seventeen minutes a page by not dunking it,
It's like he went through a barrel in a couple of squirts,
And Sam, snatching at the chance to help him, spoke up,
'Oh, dynamite! This'll show the boys sourdough at work:
John won't be obliged to skimp, I won't be tossed out
On my backside, and we'll all be off to the races.'
Sam gave his instructions with his thumb, and Ike lugged
The sourdough in tanks over to the kegs out in back
Of Inkslinger's office, shouldered the goop and slopped it
Into the pen juice: it fizzed and burbled four bars
Of Yankee Doodle, while Sam leaned on a keg, smiling,
'It's sparking up a little! It's okay, though, it'll settle.'
Kerblooey! All of the rib-splintering barrels exploded
To blue heaven with a whoosh of bamblustercation,
Flooring Ike, jolting Sam to the top of a black ridge
Of ink and sourdough, spouting across the ice fields!
The blowup plowed under a green mile of oak saplings
And when it cracked a fence close to the blacksmith's shed,
Big Ole broke out wonder-struck, still holding his hammer,
And gawking up at Sourdough Sam, riding the flood
Just like a broncobuster high-rolling with the bucks
On top of a hot sunfishing and jackknifing horse,
But he was waving a stump, and bawling at his blood.

As quick as think, big Ole strung a loop into a rope,
Circled it around his head, spilled it and lassoed Sam,
While Bunyan and the boys all galloped up in a sweat.
Inkslinger, who was a born doctor, knelt down by Sam
And talked him through the twinges as he patched him up:
'Sit tight, you high-flying mule-hearted old galoot,
And tough it out. Don't you dare sag without a tussle!
There's nothing wrong with you a lazy April won't fix,
Say a whirl on a sternwheeler down the Muddysippi,
With those tall drifting days full of old jokes and whiskey,
The sky all mare's-tail clouds, the haymaking sun high
In the sticky air, and you loafing by the rail, joy-riding
Past the green and mayfly islands in the wide waters,
Into the poker midnights where the stakes are fat
And your luck's holding, shoot! and the peacocking gals
Tugging on your arms, slow-talking and sleepy-eyed,
The stars outside rocking to a skinny harmonica,
And day breaking with the whippoorwills streaking home,
As you roll into New Orleans so all-fired husky
You're just busting to kiss the first jackass you see.'
'Oh, the whole commotion has just caught me flat-footed,
John; I guess my damn sourdough still isn't up
To scratch, and now, thanks to me, all your ink is lost.
I'm as sorry as a yellow dog with his tail tucked.'
'Forget it, whiskers. We won't let a two-bit disaster
Split up old partners like us, will we? I'd sooner lose
All the ink in Philadelphia than one Sourdough Sam.
You just build your steam back up, okay? Oh, dynamite!'
Inkslinger stood, shouldered his way past Blowhard Ike,
Who was in the middle of his sob act, wiping his nose,
And walked on over to old Paul, saying kind of soft,
'He's got a blast furnace instead of a heart: he'll pull through,
But he'll be one-armed and one-legged from here on out.'
The sun was fat, the spring thaw on, and the water falling
In Red Lake: the hour was skyrocketing toward the deadline,
And the boys were hustling like salmon to save the lumber.
Inkslinger quit dotting his i's and crossing his t's,
To stretch his last barrels of ink, and Paul signed on
Hot Biscuit Slim as the new greaseball, a red-eyed man
Who just pined away, and only spoke on cloudy Thursdays.
Slim moved into the spitnew and spanglorious cook shanty,

Which was so thumping big they handed out maps at the door,
And cranked out everything from bull steak to ice cream.
But Blowhard Ike kicked around camp, walking in the slush:
'How in the world did I get stuck in this horse opera?
I think these hicks would patch it up after an earthquake
And sail back into work: I bitch, and they start grinning;
I feel like a bullfrog in the dust bowl on a hot Sunday.'
Ike barged into the chuckhouse, where Hot Biscuit Slim
Was stirring up the lunch, and started to sweet-talk him
Into fixing up bucksaws and boots with oatmeal dough.
Slim sniffed out the polecat in back of the explosion,
And he straightened up, tugged at his cap, squinted at Ike,
Shook his head, shook it, nodded, spit an arc of tobacco,
Coiled into his windup, slanted his arm with his elbow high,
Ripped out a pitch, and knocked him out with an old doughnut.
Double-Jawed Phalen, who once went scrounging for cheese
And ate a grindstone by mistake, was the only man
Who had the tusks to bite into one of Slim's doughnuts.
When Ike woke up and hauled his headache to the door
He saw the whole cuckoo outfit loafing around Red Lake
And lumber jammed in the lake as black as a crow's eye.
Sourdough Sam was leaning on a crutch up a sugarloaf hill,
And squatting by the old cookshack, Paul Bunyan yelled:
'Spring has frisked up the stretch and beat us to the wire,
But, much obliged to Sam, we're still going to swing it,
And blow this timber out of here! Okay, Babe: let her whoop!'
Babe tugged, and the tilting cookshack, which Sam had crammed
With sourdough, went sliding rickety down the rollway:
When it hit the water there was nothing but blue hell,
The lake splurging up like a waterfall on its head,
And the logs cartwheeling down the Red River Valley!
Snatching his straw hat, Blowhard Ike broke like bad news
And faded out in the direction of Pike County, Missouri.
Slim's kitchen smells turned out so scrumdiddliumptious,
When the noon gabriel blew the boys didn't finish a stroke,
But all roared straight in, leaving their axes in mid-air.

6

In the sunburnt fall, when the light fairly thins out,
And summer's gone like a fast freight on a dream line,
And the needles jiggle on the jade pines in a slack sky,
With the Red River load all shipped off to the sawmill
And his slashers and sawyers buckling down to new work,
Paul Bunyan was out there cracking the high timber down
From Brainerd to Bemidji, across wide-ribbed Minnesota.
Brimstone Bill the bullwhacker, in buckskin and fringes,
Jogged through the haze in the air to talk to Bunyan.
'Afternoon, Bill. What's on your mind, besides pig feathers?'
'I don't know; I might be wide by a thousand miles, Paul,
I hope I am, but blast me if there ain't something ailing
Your old blue ox: it's nothing, he just ain't up to snuff.
I yoked and harnessed him, but he just hitched off, instead
Of galloping out slap-bang to the woods, like always;
He wouldn't chomp on the scrub or slurp up water nohow,
And the truth is, he didn't ram me with his horn, once.
To sling it to you straight, the ox is too damn polite,
With none of the old shenanigans, none of the fireworks;
He's as tame as a snail on a leash, and must be sick.'
Paul was walking in a flash, and Brimstone Bill behind;
They sighted the blue ox by a creek, on the near bank,
With his head stooped, his round eyes flat, and his legs shaky,
And Paul smacked him on his sky-blue flank and shouted,
'Hey, Babe! You ducking work? Won't you give me a lick?'
The big ox just snuffled, and Paul said, 'Fetch Inkslinger:
I'd like it if you'd go two steps ahead of bolt lightning.'
The sharp timekeeper cut out to the creek and snorted,
'What's new, superman? I'm almost caught up with –Hey,
Babe's sure looking seedy. Whoa, boy: hold it right there!
Look, I've stitched up your rascals after their eye-gouging
And ear-chewing fights, I've doctored them all laid up
With logger's smallpox from a Sunday stomp in the face
With a spiked boot, and I worked miracles with bellyaches,
But never in all my time moonlighting as a pill shooter
Have I treated one of your four-legged switch-tailed critters!
I'm no vet; why, I don't know the muzzle from the shank;
I'm all for fixing Babe, but you've got the wrong rooster.'
'Fake it, Johnny! Aren't you the joker who lit on a moose dead
Of old age, and tracked it clear back to its birthplace?
We're ninety miles from nowhere, you're the medicine man,

Babe's to the bad, and you won't shake your salt to help?
Lose him, make him better, but don't you let him drift!'
'Okay, okay. But I won't jump into this baldheaded:
You've got to spare me a couple of minutes to hit the books.
I mean I can't catch fire with a fishhook and all
I promise is an outside chance, but I'll give her a go.'
While Inkslinger thumbed through his headache books,
Hot Biscuit Slim fixed a batch of flapjacks and parsnips,
And Brimstone Bill carted them out to the baby-blue ox,
Who tromped on his foot like old times, but only sniffed
And licked at the vittles, and stuck by the frisky creek.
Then Johnny Inkslinger hitched out with his black bag,
Walked Babe into the stable, and started trouble-shooting
With book in hand, busy as a cowbird in a short pasture:
He poked the haunches, tested the joints, studied the blood;
He stood out in back of the blue ox with a check list
And stared at his hindquarters through an old spyglass,
Wondering what on earth could bother a bull that big.
It couldn't be a tummy-ache: once when they were swamped
With sawdust, they just strapped green goggles on the ox
And let him graze; his stomach was immortal; he could
Down a brush whiskey still without so much as a hiccup.
Six loggers were lowered by a hoist into Babe's throat
And swampers combed his hide yard by yard for a sore,
But they found nothing special, and Inkslinger was stumped.
When old Paul asked what was the story, the timekeeper
Went up and down the barn, yawping like a steam calliope:
'Yeah, just call me Sawbones! There's no virus I can't nail!
I had a hunch when your ox first went off his feed,
And now I've looked into it, I've got a big nothing!
It ain't the blind staggers, the sniffles, breakbone fever,
The jitters, heartburn, the pukes, foot-and-mouth, the whoops,
All I know's what it ain't: and it sure ain't my round.
I was out of my skull when I ever hooked into this!
Temperature? Oh boy! Heartbeat: boom boom. Breath, yikes!
I pump my head, and all for nothing: ixnay, zero, no soap!
We're miles past March, and so it can't be his old hay fever;
And there's just no dang symptoms but the hump on his back.
It's got me as puzzled as a squeal pig in a washtub.
What about the hump? If we straighten out his spine,
There's an okay chance it'll shove him back into shape;

Keep bumping, you old blue ox: you'll be skyhooting soon!'
An alley-oop crew, after sticking ladders and scaffolds
Up Babe's back, climbed up with jerk lines and grass ropes,
Inkslinger and Big Swede stood at the blue moon horns
And Bunyan manned the tail, and they pitched all their beef
Into the tug-of-war, stretching Babe like the last dollar.
Johnny flashed the high sign by and by, and the three
Turned the front-page and cosmological tall ox loose:
Babe whinnied and cavorted like a two-gun tornado,
Johnny yelled it's working, and Paul reddened with love.
But the spunky blue ox had been bluffing, and soon stood
Shivering on his hoofs, swimming, with his ribs rawboned,
His bellow sour, and the hump on his back ballooning.
Old Paul stuck his thumbs in his front pockets like a tough:
'What's next, doc? Look: we've got sixteen tons of slow blues
And no damn time. The Armstrong method got us nowhere:
I reckon you'll have to switch on the old think box.'
'Don't crowd me, big daddy: I'm thinking in six languages.
Okay, so what if I foozle, huh? Where's your miracle?
Do you know Big Ole's motto? He says, "If I can't fix it,
I just paint it yellow and send it back to the woods."
What do you say? I didn't volunteer for this whangdilly,
And you can just go play that on your tack piano!'
'Oh, my aching back, shut up, Inkslinger: shut your mouth!
No other horse doctor alive will tackle my blue ox,
Except you, you kite-flying quack! so boom, you're hired!
Don't you crawfish on me, just jump back in your shanty
And don't budge out till you get lucky! Oh, and Johnny!
I'm sorry I slammed you: I'm as touchy as a colt.'
Old Paul and Big Swede stood rubbing the blue ox down,
Waiting news, whittling time, listening to the chug of axes
In the blunt woods, where no timber moved to the Crow Wing.
When Inkslinger showed, he sidled up to Paul and said,
'Whale milk.' 'Whale milk?' 'Don't you savvy American?
It's the milk of a whale: in plain U.S., whale milk.'
'That's the cure, eh Johnny? Where do we scare up a whale?'
'We point ourselves at the tall grass, pack up our plunder,
Thumb a ride on a prairie schooner, and haul out west.'
Paul Bunyan plunked the whole camp and caboose on wheels,
And Big Ole, who could shoe six mustangs at once in his lap,
Scooped out an iron mine for Babe's shoes, and coming back

With his brawny arms full, he sank to his hips in bedrock.
With Babe hitched up, and all loaded to go, Bunyan hollered,
'Okay, let's get this circus on the road! The coast or bust!'
The camp was flying through the blizzards and swingcats
Of South Dakota when, rising out of the buck brush
On its three legs, this local beast with a gun barrel nose
Snickered, and after taking a clay bullet out of its cheek,
It cocked its head and fired. It was a rare tripodero,
And the boys showed a sudden interest in Nebraska.
Out in the yellow sandhills, they saw a sidehill dodger
At home by the Platte River, with stumps for up legs
And stilts for down, which is how it kept level, whirling
Rip around the hill with black eyes, saw teeth, hard bristles,
Yowling, burrowing, tail-spinning, and throwing kisses.
They hit the badlands in a dry spell, and way out there
In the acres of red dust, box canyons, and hot rocks,
Where only the grasshoppers and pumpkins can survive,
They found a squatter who was so thirsty the only way
He could whistle to his hound dog was to ring a bell,
And the almighty dog was so terrible wheezy and dry
It had to lean up against a rail fence just to bark.
Babe got stung by a drove of horseflies out of nowhere,
And they all left the land of blackwater and cornhuskers
When the blue ox stampeded into Colorado territory.
There they swapped brags with a contrary oil monkey,
Too old to hunt buffalo, too young to prospect silver,
Who built a derrick like a double dare to the cyclones.
His bad luck was it was as dry as a Nebraska eye;
His good luck was one Friday night the twisters came
And unscrewed the well: when he saw the thousand-foot
Hole sticking up in the air, he sliced it into hunks
And sold it east for post holes. Outside Cripple Creek
The boys took a two-beer time out, and a quick look
At the sliver cats, with their slit eyes and tasseled ears,
And their skinny tails tipped with a bone-and-spike ball:
They'd sit politely on a branch and knock a tourist out
With the bone side, and haul the catch up with the spikes.
Old Paul and Big Swede were out mudslinging, working on
A joke landmark: they slapped big rubble and wet clay
Around a pike pole, like a real mountain, called it Pike's Peak,
And rallied the boys, hotfooting it out to Wyoming,

On the hammer like old outlaws, across the Great Divide,
Where they saw a turkey-headed green-necked goofus bird,
With a red wing flipping and a black wing flopping,
Hooting, spiralling in the air out of its upside down nest,
Flying backwards all the way to Cheyenne and gone
Because it only loves to look at wherever it's been.
Babe got thirsty, and with no water in sight, old Paul
Took a pickax and whopped the glory out of the ground,
And when the water spouted, and Babe was sipping it,
Wham, the spring shut off, and bam, it shot off regular,
And so Bunyan named the fountain Old Faithful, in honor
Of the blue ox, but after a swig, renamed it Old Filthy.
He figured on turning south for the sun, on account
Of the blue ox shivering in the cool and the sagebrush,
And the boys thumbed their noses at the poor sheepherders,
And then wheeled through the lilies and beehives of Utah.
Coming through the salt flats, and avoiding the joint snakes,
Which split in twelve and strike everywhichway at once,
With its wheels kicking up copper clouds, the logging camp
Crossed over the mesas into Arizona, where it's painted
With six coats of sundown, and the weather report is fire.
It was so mythological hot, for example, a lean coyote
Was chasing a jack rabbit, and they were both walking,
Fish in the arroyos made puffs of dust as they swam,
And natives, who could hardly mix a pitcher of lemonade
Before night, saw flu-flu birds splashing in mirage lakes.
Bunyan, hailing from the North country, was breathing hard
With the heat, and he lowered his peavey and let it drag,
Plowing the hollow which was later called the Grand Canyon.
They dawdled in Nevada, hoping for just a peekaboo
At the three-tailed bavalorous, with a crooked horn
On its forehead, bird body to its hips, with shaggy legs
And starry hoofs, and then the world-famous three tails:
The first a harpoon, sharp as a Green Mountain winter,
The second a branch, doubling as a brace and a whip,
The third a galaxy, sprawling, all flash and feathers,
And perched proudly over its left shoulder for show.
They skittered the sage hens, looked at the glory diggings,
And shoved on to California, with weather eyes out
For gold and grizzlies, and old Babe was perking up now
Like a brass band quickstepping down Main on turkey day.

Paul Bunyan jumped the Sierras, and landing on the outskirts
Of the sequoias and stealing in there by his lonesome,
He leaned against twenty centuries, looking for words:
'Oh hit me with a hayseed, and lay me in the clover:
I'd say you were flapdoodle if I couldn't slap bark,
Redwoods. I reckon you were shooting when the sea was
First slopping, standing the winters here, in the haggle
Of storks and buzzards, green with the knack of surviving,
And now you cram the sky, as old as stargazing, high
As a farm boy full of moonshine. You're the bluest berry
On the fat earth, I wouldn't fall you for dare or double.
Whee! I like, –oh my, I'd best let the bluejays tweet
My thanks to creation, now: I'm fresh out of tall talk.'
The lumber camp had barged across the Oregon border,
Where they saw a teakettler walking backwards, whistling
And blowing steam out its red nose. At south coast camp,
They swapped their axes for idiot sticks to shovel out
Inkslinger's whale corral, and carved Coos Bay, as Babe
The blue ox was rickety as a calf, and sick all over.
Old Paul slogged out to sea, whinnying to the grey world
And croaking to the whales in kind of salt-water Greek,
Till Dynamite Jack, who was up a tree in a crow's nest,
Sighted flukes and spouts and yodeled There she blows,
And a blue gang of sperm whales dove in the whale corral,
As thick as whores at a horse race, and the way old Paul
Was blubbering, it was dumb luck he didn't sing half
The hogs in three counties into his big arms to boot.
Big Swede, the North Sea all-star milking champ, walked in
Swinging his bucket, and with his fists full of whale tits
He stood there, squishing and yanking like a steam pump,
Duded up in his cowboy jeans and his ten-gallon hat,
Catching the spew in the pail tight between his knees:
'Whoopee-ti-yi-yo! I'm an old Chisholm cowpoke, boys!
Daddy was a mule skinner, mama was a man-eater!
Oh, I was born in the saddle, suckled on beer, and I'm dusty;
I'm a long horn, I'm a blue moon, and I'm full of fleas;
I've got pig iron bones and thirteen rows of jaw teeth;
I root and toot, punch cows, I ride slick, and knock down!
Whoa, boy! Sing to me, six-guns! Yippee-ki-yi-yay!'
The pail was brimming with luscious milk in no time;
Inkslinger waded out and said, 'Calm down, buckaroo,'

Fetched it on back to the beach where the blue ox lay,
And sat joshing with Bunyan while Babe set to lapping:
'The boy's a caution! Where does he get that foofaraw?
He's never wrangled horses, wrestled steers, or rolled his own!'
Old Paul didn't hear him: the blue ox at the big bucket
Was slumping, drooling, sick of milk, with his wind hard
And his blue eyes scummed with fear. On the plain sand
Bunyan rounded up his boys, under an unclear sky,
In a fine drizzle, by the slop and bash of the waves:
'It's no good, boys. Babe's dying. He's tough, but so what?
White pines in the steady sun, brook trout in blue water,
Owls sliding out on the weather, bulls steaming in the mud,
You mopping the kitchen, your honey going for the mail, are
All equal, all dripping with risk, like icicles in April.
It's a skinny consolation, at a funeral. Now my beauty
Is buckling, oh brother! in death, in one jump nothing
But a tall tale, and all my love's curdling in my belly.
It's a raw afternoon, where's the campfire? It's crazy,
But morning, without my companion, will go on breaking.'
He took a shovel that was handy, and stumped up the coast
To gouge out a grave for the blue ox. Inkslinger snorted,
'Oh hold on a minute, boys; services ain't started yet:
I'm still scratching! Now if whale milk won't clear it up,
Why, dang it, all of this aggravation is in his head!
Big Swede, plunk yourself down in front of the fool ox,
Eye to eye, and say "You're okay, Babe," over and over,
And don't quit for high tide or red indians, follow me?
If we just buck him up, he'll be healthy as a seesaw.'
Big Swede cinched his cowboy hat and sat by the ox:
'You're okay, Babe. You're okay, Babe. You're okay, Babe.
Oh, Mister Inkslinger says so. And I say so, big Babe.
You're okay. You're okay, big Babe. You're okay, big Babe.'
He chittered and chattered, and in a while it was like
Saying hoop-de-doodle: the words were nothing but babble;
He spouted it like an old song, and it wore his voice down
To a wheeze, but a swig of whiskey would fix him up,
And he whisked out a crate of Inkslinger's white lightning,
Oiled his tonsils on the half hour, and went on droning
At the blue ox. He was on his thirteenth bottle, when
He flared up, with his eyes popping, and fire alarms
In his ears, drunk as a rainbow trout, and he hooted,

'Oh, you sick ox. Whoop! Oh Babe! Whoop! You dumb ox.'
He was swacked: the beach was swinging all round his head,
And Big Swede, looking out at the water romping, burped
And rolled to his back, with a pile of seaweed for a pillow,
And tipping the crate over; whiskey pooled on the sand,
And old Babe licked it up, stamped into Johnny's shack,
Ate up a ton of pills, and cavorted. His bounce was back.
He waddled off, sniffing for Bunyan, but the white lightning
Hit him between the horns, and he lurched off the trail,
Curling back south to Crater Lake, snorting in the cold.
The sprinkle of rain sifting down on the green country
Thickened, and thunder coughed all across the flat sky,
While the blue ox, plumb lost, on the lookout for Bunyan,
Shoved on, with his ramshackle heart rocking with love.
The tall clouds cracked and it rained like all hickory,
Babe hobbling nowhere in the black mud, and the spray
Spitting off his tail was building into the Rogue River,
Till up on a mistletoe hill, the weather unwinding,
The blue ox slammed sideways onto the grass and died.
Old Paul came into camp and chased out with Inkslinger,
Hunting up his ox down south, clear to California:
When he sighted the carcass on the hill, he folded his arms
Over his belly, and stooped down under the white sun.
Inkslinger stood there like a haystack, rubbing his arm,
And scared of the streaks on the puddles. Water dangled.
It was windy up on Mount Shasta, blowing down
To the west, and a whoosh of air went fanning across
The hill, wagging the dandelions all around the dead ox.
After one whiff, the blue ox was alive and sashaying.
Bunyan whistled and hugged him off his hoofs, shouting,
'I love you, California: I ain't kidding, your air is fresh!'
Johnny was cussing hard, jumping like at a hoedown,
Babe bucked, and pastured in an acre of parsnips,
And old Paul heehawed like a Rocky Mountain canary.

7

Winter barged in early with a spell of weather as cold
As the windy side of an Idaho tombstone by happy
New year starlight, and the sun went south with the geese.
The North country only had three seasons: July, August,
And winter, and when it dipped down to sixty-odd feet
Below zero, the loggers couldn't light a wood match
On a grindstone, the pot of java froze up so fast
It was still steaming, and the boys sucked on the ice,
And when the tin can lantern flames froze, the cooks said
To twist them off the wicks, and crush them up for pepper.
The blue ox, out walking with hay bales and feed sacks
On his wide horns, had got a hayseed stuck in his ear,
And when Brimstone Bill, who was up a pine to reach it,
Yelled out for a ladder down, since it was too slick,
Paul Bunyan told him to piss and slide down on the icicle.
It was so awful chilly, talk froze in the crackling air,
And the lumberjacks walked around bumping into words;
And the spring thaw was like a bull shooting contest,
With cracks defrosting all over the evergreen camp:
'Howdy Oh meow and nuts Go ahead So what Timber
It ain't weather it's a disease Ho hum Good enough
Screw you punk In the kitchen with Dinah What gives
I'm champ Okay sweetheart Says who Get the shovel
It's sky-bound Gee It beats me Haw Take it easy.'
Big Swede, gallivanting across the slow snowdrift
Where the skid road lay, saw this loose whiplash there,
Brimstone Bill's by the braid of it, and when he stooped
For it, it yanked out of his paws, and Bill roared up,
'Let go, you dirty five-fingered damn chicken thief,
I'm hauling a hundred tons of butt log in bad weather
Back of two teams of mean oxen, and I need the lash!'
Yeah, Washington was cold, and the snow deep as the world.
Pumphandle Joe stretched out, with a yawn and a sniff,
Hitched up his bay pony to a bush, and took a nap.
He snoozed clean through the thaw: when he woke up,
He saw his horse dangling from a limb of a Douglas fir.
Old Paul had never seen the likes of this west coast timber;
It was clear and fat, it was so thick a hummingbird
Would snag in it, and tall to where it took two loggers
To see up to the top: oh, it was a green daydream.
Bunyan knocked over a yellow pine for a creek bridge,

And Brimstone Bill, poking the oxen across it, kept on
Coming up shy by a couple after every crossing.
He would've heard them splash for sure if the dumb cows
Were drowning, and likewise he would've spotted a rustler;
He fished all around, and found them in the hollow trunk
Of the big yellow pine: they'd slipped through the knotholes.
Cedar Root Charley and Rocky Dan had tackled a tree
Which was sticking up through a hole in the calico sky,
With falling axes and a great stack of crosscut saws
Brazed into one, chewing up bark, gobbling up sawdust
For ages and ages, and when they were dry and winded,
They sneaked around the pine tree for a snort of whiskey
And saw who on earth but Roaring Jim and Billy the Bum,
In their red shirts and blue jeans, working the far side,
Swapping big lies, old-time gags, pigtails of tobacco,
And whanging away at the same honest-to-god tree.
The rollways went up on the shore of the Jack Off River,
Which flowed as sleek as a kiss, as choppy as a punch,
And liked to duck under and bob up like a fool rabbit,
Full of snags and loggers, and maybe a whirl or three;
Splitting up, zigzagging, squirting on, humping itself,
It squiggled and galumphed to the rub-a-dub ocean,
Slap into Puget Sound, the grave old Paul had dug
For the blue ox, wide open for all the whopping logs
Booming over the cockeyed river, and the cockeyed roads,
Which were so crooked the poor skidders couldn't tell
If they were riding out somewhere or on their way home,
And when a jack met himself coming back from the landing
It was time to hook up Babe and jerk out the kinks.
Now what with the cold weather, large trees, and bad river
They had in that late Northwest midwinter afternoon,
Nothing short of a rip-roaring fire-eating man could
Manage it, and so a wrangler, name of Old Lightheart,
Dragged a bunch of scissorbills off the farms to the east,
And changed them from hay shakers into buffalo boys:
He lit into his saddle tramp pitch and sold them all,
Stripped off their sheep-stinking laundry, dressed them up
In buckskin duds, bandannas, and buzzard wing chaps,
And set his boys to circle herding, lasso looping, guitar
Picking, and buffalo milking out in the pine-rail corral.
Old Lightheart's whole notion was that a barrel a man

Of this here hair-curling and bare-chested buffalo milk
Would give the lumberjacks the go for all-out logging.
There wasn't a glass of milk or a doughnut but was spiked
With it, and Jersey lightning was branch water next to it.
The boys took to raw bear meat topped off with the bones,
And whipped off their mackinaws, joking about the cold;
They razzed each other till they all turned rantankerous,
Throwing ax handle parties, leaking blood; they showed off
By skinning the cat on a long branch on a tall pine,
Grabbing sky, and somersaulting down on the Cascades.
The buffalo boys took a slug of the milk all around,
Rode out in wolf-skin coats, looking for buck-jumping colts,
And out front was Old Lightheart, on a mountain lion,
Riding bareback and screaming for American cows.
The hardtail winter broke up into a freak spring,
Rainy and crazy, like a pool hustler on a bad night,
And Slabwood Johnson, thinking the woods pretty damp
And waddling into a clearing, saw all kinds of rain.
Water alone wouldn't flutter his feathers, he could take
A drizzle; it wouldn't have flustered him at all, but
It was raining straight up, squirting out of the mud
Into a sky blue as the blue ox on a blue morning.
He went swooping like a gander for the big bunkhouse
But the floor was as full of cracks as a Yankee peddler
To let out slush and such from the spiked logging boots,
And so the water spattered into the room by the bucket,
And naturally the roof was so watertight the rain
All puddled overhead, and when Slabwood skipped in
He bumped into a god-damn upside down hog wallow.
He bounced back out into the hazy sunlight and ran
Red-faced to Paul's shanty, clucking like a prairie hen.
'Okay, Bunyan! You see this slop all over my kisser?
I walked into the bunkhouse and I forgot to duck!
It's no fair, sweetheart! Hey, why ain't it raining in here?'
'Simmer down, Slabwood! You bang in here without knocking,
And start handing out birdseed till I'm woozy as you:
Jenny's pass, no savvy, I don't know, and all that.
Now back up to the bunkhouse part, and if you feel
Conflabberation coming over you, take a couple of hoots
Of this here horse liniment. All right, what's eating you?'
'I'll tell you flat, Bunyan. Get this: it's raining up.'

'Oh, now you're logging! You mean a storm's clabbering up.'
'If I do, sweetheart, you can plant me out on the plains
For buffalo chow. I mean the rain isn't falling: no,
The rain is falling, but backwards; I mean it's flying,
It's coming down antigoglin to the ground, hold it,
I'm wrong! I'm wrong! Aw, hell. Where's the horse liniment?'
Old Paul was smiling out the window: a whingding of rain
Was coming up from China, and when he whipped back
His big bearskin rug, the water spindled into the air.
Slabwood was cackling to himself, hoisting the bottle,
When Inkslinger dropped in for a powwow, and old Paul
Handed him a cup of java and a question mark.
'I'll tell you, old scout: the lowdown is, the camp's hurting.'
Johnny poured a streak of moo into the bellywash,
Sugared it up to kill the taste, and tried explaterating:
'The boys are twitchy, the cooks are sulky, the blue ox
Is acting silly, Slim is his usual self, and I've got
My eye on a peach farm way out in South Carolina.
This new-fangled rain, yikes! Oh I know, you were low
On coffee, and so you boiled up a handful of turds!
As I was saying, this Yankee trick out of the sky,
I mean the mud, is giving our camp the jumps, man,
And if we don't get to finagling, we might as well
Call it a bust and go slop hogs in Dixie Land.'
Bunyan leaned out the door and yelled at the West coast:
'Okay, I can see the weather's screwed up out here!
Wise up, you turkeys; I mean if it's raining backwards,
Saw backwards, or whatever: don't let it crack you up!
The first clown I catch sneaking back to the bunkhouse,
Watch out! I'm going to inspect his guts by hand!
You boys keep the pines shaking, I can beat the water!'
He slumped down by Johnny and rippled through a wish book.
'We could wrap them up real heavy, Bunyan, but hell,
It seems like clothes are figured for everyday rain
And all shed water down, just like shingles on a roof;
But this dang rain jumps up your blue jeans, your slicker,
Your favorite shirt, your long underwear, your beaver hat,
Into your hip pockets, under your belt, down your socks,
And you squish off with the Great Lakes in your work shoes,
And soaked to the leather: whoo! it's a sin to Crockett,
And no wonder the boys are ugly. Ha, if you could

Haul your britches on upside down, you'd be okay!'
'Hush up, Johnny; look here in this mail-order catalogue:
Quilts, rockers, silverware, trombones, tubs, umbrellas!
I want a boxcar of umbrellas: write me up an order.'
'Yeah, but they ain't worth a whistle in this weather!
Who's going to want to lug around his own puddle?
I say we order up a tub of booze and a holiday.'
Old Paul clapped up the wish book and sneered like a horse:
'You stop yapping, and stamp it rush: I've got an angle.'
When Brimstone Bill saw a shipment of umbrellas come
Jolting into camp, he jumped on his hat and sneezed,
Gave a yodel to the barn boss, and waved him over:
The barn boss had been contemplating how to shovel
Babe's crap out of the swampers' way, when the up rain
Sprinkled into the pile, which commenced to steam,
And the stink turned his whiskers as white as an egg.
The bullwhacker showed him the umbrellas, and they hiked
Over to Paul's office, with the barn boss looking prickly
And Brimstone Bill spitting out words like apple seeds:
'Thanks a million for the parasols, dear! I picked
A bunch of daffodils to go with them, and they're darling.
I'm going to wear them in my butt! Oh, why fight it!
Unpack the petticoats, handsome: let's dance ourselves silly!
And get this, jelly bean: you can take your shower sticks
Out of your boxcar, and shove them up your caboose!
My pal here will help you. I'll take rain any way you
Throw it before I'll slink around under an umbrella!'
Old Paul smiled like a coon up a sugar tree and said,
'You yokels have been hitting the buffalo milk too hard,
You're thinking with your fists. Yeah, umbrellas are okay
For old ladies who won't look the weather in the face,
But hell, I'd rather swim than pretty you boys up, so
Get off of your high horse: this ain't that kind of rodeo.
Go ahead and grab you a couple of bumbershoots
And bust off the handles, strap on rawhide and bang!
You've got rain shoes. Try them on, lollipop: they work!'
The boys latched on to the rain shoes like easy money,
And Brimstone Bill was out there getting the hang of his
When Old Lightheart whistled up to him in a sweat:
'Hey, man; I was out spelunking in a hole yonder
When I burnt my fingers, bobbled my fire, and whoa!

I heard a squalling like it's the granddaddy buffalo,
And skedaddled. Tell Paul, while I keep an eye out here.'
The bullwhacker bumped into Inkslinger and yelled,
'Say, will you hunt up Bunyan; tell him Old Lightheart
Was out prospecting when he flopped into a dry gulley,
His arm caught fire, he let go his handful of daylight,
And he was trampled by buffalo under a stiff rain.'
Old Paul was in his shanty when Johnny showed and said,
'Guess who's up to his elbows in trouble: Old Lightheart
Struck it rich up on Sawtooth Ridge, spilled off a cliff,
On fire, burned like a weed in the flat sky, blacked out,
Slammed down out of the rain and was squashed by a cow.'
'Come on, Johnny: don't you give me your ten-story lies,
Because I ain't buying. I want a fish and a yardstick:
Let's see Old Lightheart, and get the honest-to-god.'
When the buffalo boy was done pointing and exaggerating,
Bunyan rammed square into the cave, but it was like
Trying to get a rooster into a game of checkers,
And so he snuggled up, listened till he was popeyed,
Hooted into the dark, and swayed up onto his feet:
'Boys, there's only one animal can make such a ruckus
Of banging and shimmering, and it's a kid rainstorm
Hollering mama, strayed and holed up under our camp,
Spooked, and raining like silly, which is why it's coming
Up! If we could persuade the maverick out of the cave,
We could start towelling off: it's a cinch we can't haul
Weather around by the tail, as there's no tail to grab;
But if I dress up like his mom, in big raindrops,
I can thunder and lullaby him clear to the Plains.'
Inkslinger didn't blink, but just cocked back his hat:
'Okay, dreamer; I'm sticking around for this: first,
Where the hell in Hicktown USA are you going to get
The outfit? I mean, they must be sold out everywhere.'
'I hear there's nothing you can't buy in Kansas City.'
'Well how, buck-naked and soaking wet, you going to make
A hunk of cloud, which is as bashful as a barn swallow,
Believe you're its own mom, instead of an ad gimmick?'
Paul was lurching toward Missouri when he shouted back,
'I guess I'll just have to work up a solid routine!'
Inkslinger gave the boys the screwball sign and said,
'There's times when I could swear I was in a dime novel,

But then I shine up my memory, and I snap out of it:
Like now, ask me who in the whole showboating country
Can walk out and flimflam a rainstorm, and I'll say
Oh, a lumberjack, tall as the Sierras, and heading east.'
It took a lot of looking, but old Paul rounded up
A true Kansas City hustler, squinting at the yokels,
With a rose in his coat and a suitcase full of steals.
Bunyan walked up behind him, and whistled at his back:
'Hey man, start pitching: I want to rent a disguise.'
The dude twirled on his boot heels and fell on the grass,
And in a minute, when he woke up, he smiled at Bunyan:
'Oh my but you startled me, son, with your big howdy!
Oh, oh! And behind my back! It's funny; but you know,
You can't carry a weapon in lots of these bible belt towns,
And son, my advice to you is this: use sign language.
I sell eye to eye, so I'll have to bargain with you
From here, flat on my back: you just stand still, okay?
You're real tall, son! Yeah, you take after the North Star!
And you want a disguise! Oh yeah, I can picture it:
We'll get you a white hat and a couple of yucca trees,
And you can pass as Mount Whitney. Why don't you yell,
Scratch that: why don't you point at what in creation
It is you want to look like? You're pointing at what,
At a rain cloud! And you're not laughing. How about you
Forget the disguise, and let me sell you a box of matches?
I could throw in a bottle of hair shine; oh all right,
Don't get your back up! I can handle it, don't panic:
I just hope you brought a hat full of greenbacks, is
All I can say, on account of this is a special order
As your cloudburst outfits don't come in extra large.
Okay: we've got your basic sprinkle, but I imagine
You're looking for a downpour, and as for cloud structure,
It would be just too crude to wear cumulus in society,
Since anyone who's anyone's in nimbus this season.
And, let's see, in our April line, though you might fancy
A light shower, no charge for the thunder, I suggest
A root-searching rain, which is the only style I carry.
Oh, shall I wrap it, or should I go get my umbrella?'
Old Paul stared down at the tiny salesman and snapped,
'I ain't got all day, speed: just get my merchandise.'
He plunked down a stack of money and clouded over,

Fired off a snort of thunder and a couple of swipes
Of chain lightning, and floated out west in a tail wind.
When he saw a hawkeye squatting out on the prairie
And hoeing corn, it showed him he was on top of Iowa,
Where the rainstorms summer, and old Paul kicked around
With a crowd of them, who figured him for a stranger
Blown up from the Gulf. He sang and roughhoused with them
At all their get-togethers, getting their lingo straight,
And raining out political rallies like an old-timer.
On the far side of the Rockies, Brimstone Bill, standing
Hip deep in Green River mud, was poking sugar pines
And flapping off the rain, inventing new swear words
For the rolling crew, when a hoop snake with its tail in
Its mouth came skimming like a wheel out of the bushes.
Bill dove through the hoop to stump it, when its tail flared
And the sidewinder was gone, its sting in Bill's log wrench,
Which swelled up so big the boys were looking for saws
When an axhandle hound, with a hatchet head, scooted
Out of who knows where, and with a woof and a tail wag
It chomped on its supper, the twelve-foot peavey handle.
Brimstone Bill grunted and slogged over to tell Inkslinger
He was off to join the circus, when a zigzag of lightning
Trimmed his whiskers and lit Inkslinger's boots on fire
With a ruckus like the buffalo boys on a Saturday night:
'Whiz poof zip creak crackle clatter tick tick tick ding
Pop slam bang boom rattle pow wham bam thank you ma'am:'
It was Paul Bunyan, sky-walking up on stilts of air,
Yahooing out of the east, and talking American thunder,
With his wet hands full of Missouri water, tossing bolts
Like horseshoes, blocking the sun with intentions of rain,
And piling up clouds till they slopped down forty ways.
Inkslinger, fooled at first, stuck his arm up in the sky
And shook hands with Bunyan, who slacked off to a mist:
'Okay, star! Let's go and see if the kid likes the show.'
Old Paul lay down to whoosh and spatter into the hole
Like ma calling, and all of a sudden the up rain stopped:
Brimstone Bill wiped his eyes, and at the very next holler
The heifer storm jumped out into the daylight and lit up
On Paul's shoulder, where it sat, looking pale and grouchy;
And with a rainy word and the directions home, old Paul
Slapped it on its rump, and it floated out of the pines
And puffed away towards Iowa, shooting off rainbows.

8

The loggers broke pine and bucked it till almost summer
On the banks of the Onion, with the water rats sliding it
On down the river full steam to the sawdust factory;
The trouble was the wild onions all along the shore
Would split open and then, when a lumberjack was blind,
He'd work on in the damn dark, with his hands full of tears
And his ax whizzing, but when the whole daffy show was
On the point of stalling, the boys asked for Paul Bunyan.
After a minute of headwork, old Paul said the idea
Was to yank out the tearjerkers, and hold a duck feed
For the gang later on, since they were all swamp angels
And green timber heroes, and hungry. Hot Biscuit Slim
Hopped to it, in his white apron, bitching and baking,
But Cream Puff Fatty wondered what to use for ducks.
Old Paul promised to scare him up a couple of thousand,
And tottered off without his gun. While he was gone,
Inkslinger was rummaging around the big kitchen
On the lookout for cookies, and saw Sour Face Murphy
Up on a stool, peeling spuds into a bucket of water,
And Sour Face was so ugly the water was fermenting.
Inkslinger saw it fizzling, walked up and took a whiff
Of true whiskey, and he hired Sour Face as a still.
Out the greasy window, Bunyan was strolling into camp
Tugging fifty-odd wagons, all full of quacking ducks,
And the bottle washers crowded him, asking how on earth
He'd bagged that many ducks that quick without a shot.
When you're a sharpshooter, he'd said, it's nothing to squat
All day in a pole thicket like a chicken on Sunday,
Your whiskey gone, your dog mixed up, and your boots wet,
And blow ducks out of the dull sky, it's just no thrill:
And leaving his popgun behind, he'd leaned into the sky,
Bawled out his name, and the ducks up and surrendered.
Oh yeah, he'd said: advertising! It always works.
The cooks were sailing, the stoves on fire, and the kitchen
Shaking, brighter than a rodeo, loud as independence:
The bread was done before a man could circle the oven,
There was water spitting, butter boiling, smoke starting,
Oh and the smell of supper was in the air for miles.
It took two savages to blow one hoot on the old horn,
And when the music hit the pines the boys climbed on
By swinging a leg over, like in the pony express,

And rode bareback on the horn's echo all the way home,
Singing off-key, and busting the cookshack door down.
The lumberjacks sat and dove straight into the greens
In wooden bowls, with love apples, American cheese,
Salt pork and the house dressing, choice of alphabet soup,
Garden sauce stew, wish wash, and the kitchen mystery,
With suds and soda crackers, triple-decker sandwiches,
Yellow baskets of johnny cake, hard biscuits, sour rolls,
With cow grease, bear sign, red horse, birdseye tenderloin,
And the main dish, in wings and drumsticks, roast duck,
With chestnuts and oranges, and duck soup on the side.
The boys played with the string beans, squash and cauliflower,
But the plain peas and corn on the cob were as popular
As pie, and the tall cakes, the old-fashioned doughnuts,
The white ice cream and the hot cookies were sloshed down
With milk out of pitchers and good coffee by the gallon.
The Galloping Kid, behind a team of ponies, shook
The reins and drove the salt and pepper wagon across
The table, hauling fruit pits, coffee grounds, and eggshells
Out to toss to the tigermonks, who got so strong on
This trash, they took to wrestling blond wolves for fun.
The grub fight went on and on, but the boys were winning,
And Cream Puff was cheering when he dropped his mixing spoon:
It sure looked like Hot Biscuit Slim had cracked a smile.
Now it had been brush ape etiquette since way back when
To shut up during chow, and worry about the groceries,
And so when Bunyan started to spout off out of nowhere,
It was flabbergasting at first, and threw everybody:
'I'll give you boys odds of a hundred to one you don't know
About my wild brothers; you ain't blind, I said brothers:
I mean my kid brothers, Soar Bunyan, the fisherman
And the big drunk, and Cal S. Bunyan, the railroad star.
Now Soar had a champion bowwow, name of Slow Music,
The all-around hound dog, who'd look up at his boss
In the morning, and if old Soar was carrying his rifle,
Slow Music went scouting for deer, if it was his shotgun
He'd sniff out rabbits, and if his fishing pole, worms.
This hound was not dumb; one time Soar was bragging how
Slow Music, like a sure enough hawk, would point at fish,
When the dog froze; Soar was on the ball in a flash,
Catching the fish in question, and when he cut it open

If there wasn't a bird inside, there's no liars in Dixie.
One day Slow Music streaked it, barking like he was crazy,
After a fox maybe, and bolting clear up Saddle Mountain,
Around Blaze Spur, on down King's Creek, and back to camp,
Where he hit a swamp ax by accident and so dang hard
It sliced him in two; Soar slapped him together quick,
But sewed him up with his left legs up, right legs down.
It didn't hurt the old hound; he kept on like all getout,
And when his legs got tuckered out he'd just whirl over
On his fresh pair, rest and keep rolling at the same time,
And now nothing in the woods could outrun Slow Music.
Soar fished northern waters all year, and in all weathers
He'd be out there at sunup, red-eyed, in his hip boots,
Drunk as a dollar, skimming flies across a puddle,
Wearing his lucky shirt and holding out for breakfast,
Whistling, and waking up the fish, thinking about girls.
He was good-looking as an actor, almost always broke,
And famous for hooking imaginary fish all by himself,
Like the goofang, swimming backwards to keep the water
Out of its eyes, around as big as a sunfish, only bigger,
And when he hoisted his the creek fell a couple of feet;
Like the whirligig fish, swimming in circles all winter, so
Soar rubbed the ice holes with bacon fat and the fish
Got worked up good, till they corkscrewed into the air
And dropped into his hands; it was a tougher job than
Catching giddy fish, which were miniature and goofy,
And would go dodging east, west, and crooked in crowds;
Soar just banged one solid to start him into bouncing,
The school copied him, till every last fish was flopping
Out of the water, oh heavens, there was nothing to it!
Soar was always scratching around for easy fishing,
Like when he tried the eastern trick on a brook trout,
Curling his fingers under its belly and then just barely
Tickling it, so it rose up toward the air peaceable;
He kept on till its back almost broke out of the water,
When he yanked hard, and sailed the fish clear to the bank.
There's the time he was still-fishing off of the rocks
When a fish hawk, flying out of the hills, dove in,
Scooped up a salmon, and hit out over Soar's head;
He gawked upward with a green eye, and clapped his hands,
And bang! the hawk let go the salmon with a skreak,

And Soar just crowed as the fish plopped into his basket.
One day in a light canoe, with a pal at the paddles,
And trailing his line out back, Soar hooked into a trout,
Husky and mean, who beat the water and wrestled him hard:
Since Soar didn't care to horse him and maybe lose him,
He tied up his pole, let the big fish tow them back across
The calm cove, and had his pal bait his hook for trolling,
And they caught two rainbows simple as they rolled home.
He had witnesses the morning he caught a lake trout
With the fool idea of taming it somehow or other;
It tickled the boys, but once he was all for a project
Argufying was silly, because there's no give up in him,
And that trout did look like it knew its geometry.
He unhooked it, let it splash in the water in his boat,
And hauled for shore, where he rolled out an apple barrel
And dunked it in the lake, and in went the little fish:
He'd been careful to catch it young, since it was clear
There'd be no teaching it if it was old and cranky.
The trout did okay swimming around in the big barrel,
And every night, when it was sleeping, he'd tiptoe up
In his stocking feet, the moon still out, jiggle the knot
Out of the knothole, and let a spurt or so of water
Out of the apple barrel: the fish had no suspicion,
And in a month it was living it up on the dry bottom.
He broke it of the barrel by sticking it out mornings
In the wet grass, and soon it could go it in the shade
Till noon o'clock: by now it was as tame as a tulip,
And the sun hardly bothered it; it tagged after him
Everywhere, down the sawdust trails and into saloons.
Appleknockers hollered, millionaires knocked themselves out
To buy it for the circus, and kids would come for miles,
But he'd shake his head, snatch his hat, whistle to his pal
And clear out, the trout waggling up the street behind him.
One day he struck out for the spring in back of his camp,
To inspect his still, stretch out, and sample his lightning;
The fish tailed him through the thin trees, into the clearing,
On the log bridge, and when he was stooping over his boiler
He heard a splash; it was nothing to him till he figured
And lurched up, too late: the trout had slipped into the creek
Through a crack in the logs, and it drowned at his feet.
He was sad, but it would have flunked winter anyhow.

He bucked himself up by rowing out on a big little pond
With a full jug of flapdoodle whiskey, fishing for bass
And fighting off the skeeters: old Soar would take a whiff,
Hook up a worm, flip it out, sit waiting for a twitch,
And reel it in, when he'd take a real crack, hook up a worm,
Flip it out, take a nice hoot, sit waiting for a twitch,
And reel it in, when he'd take a long pull, hook up a minnow,
Take a good jolt, and one for luck, flip it out, sit waiting
For a twitch, slopping it down, till a skeeter'd bite him
And fly off, bumping into trees, lit up like a steamboat.
Now with the fish stealing all his bait, his dander was up
And puzzling over it in a circular way from the booze,
He swirled a minnow in his private moonshine, hooked it
And slung it, watched a brawl broil in the green water
Till his boat rocked like in bad rapids, and guess what
He saw when he hauled it in: the minnow had the bass
By the throat, and was swinging it like a true wrestler.
Soar let him go, and cramming the bass into his creel,
Lay back for a shot of his knockdown mountain dew.
He was always too cockeyed drunk to be shy of taking
Chances, which is why he'd go scouting for cougarfish,
All claws and appetite, but it was tricky: he went so far
As to set hard money on their heads, but they laid low,
And no matter how many flies twinkled, none were fooled.
The log gar was a real beast, a joker and a bulldozer:
When it was famished it would knock a hole in the boat
With its saw-tooth snout, and Soar never hit on a hook,
In brass or steel, it couldn't snap like a salt pretzel;
But talk about slow fishing, look at the upland trout:
It was a tree nester, flying all around the old jungle,
Over not under the water; it tasted wonderful fried
But was too sly for fishermen. Folks tried to bullshit him
Into thinking it was a bird, but he wouldn't fall for it.
Now, the payoff's like this: he stomped out in the dark
South of the forty-eighth parallel, chanced on a river,
Squinted across and hoped he was equal to jumping it:
He walked up a fair size hill for a scramble start,
Streaked for the water, hit and stepped up into the sky,
And halfway there he calculated out a fall shortage
And jumped again, landing in the weeds on the far shore.
He was hankering for a snooze, and stuck his tackle box

On a limb, he thought, but next morning it wasn't there:
He looked here and yonder for maybe a bear till sundown
And there it was, hanging up on a horn of the moon.
His trouble all started when a teardrop of his home-brew
Kicked him back off balance and a beauty of a cliff:
The bottle was bashed, and the whiskey dug a Great Lake,
But Soar was in his hip boots, and when he slammed down
He bounced, and higher and higher, till he was a dot,
And that's that: anything else you hear's phoney, except
If there's fish where he is, believe me, he ain't starving.
I figure it was back around umpteen forty-eleven
When Cal dreamed up his railroad; and he proposed a line
So colossal it would outshine the Wabash Cannon Ball,
And he'd grab headlines like the brass hats and big wheels.
When he was money-raising at the ballyhoo lectures
He talked dimensions that'd amaze all the gum chewers,
And when he was bankrolled, wham! he was out on the job,
Baldheaded, full of salt, and bawling for the impossible.
It was somewheres a couple of hoots from a whistle stop
He launched into spreading out gravel and laying track
On the Ireland, Jerusalem, Australia and Southern Michigan
Railroad, which was nicknamed the I'm Just A Super Man,
But which everyone called the Eagle Line, after the engine.
Old Cal had billions of six-ton Rocky Mountain boulders
Shipped in for rocks and gravel, cut ties from California pine,
And after two hard years the country's best steel mill,
Working a thirty-six-hour day and a nine-day week,
Finished the first of the rails of the Eagle's track,
And it was laid with pile drivers beating in the spikes.
Oh he had a swell time looking for machinery giant
Enough just to work on his locomotive and his coaches,
And so he used a big pair of ferris wheels for a lathe,
A merry-go-round for a boring mill, who knows how
But he rigged up an old roller coaster as a drill press,
And since the rivets and the staybolts in the Eagle's box
Were ten yards wide, they got them hot in prairie fires,
And hammered them in by shooting cannons at them.
It was a high iron horse with razzle-dazzle wheels;
The smokestack was stupendous, the cylinders gorgeous,
The side sheets pure silver, the crown sheet solid gold,
The big bell was the very image of the Liberty Bell,

The journal box was famous, the air brakes wonderful,
The cowcatcher would handle a day herd of longhorns,
And the whistle could sing I've Been Working on the Railroad.
Now when the mud chickens were all done drawing pictures,
And the powder monkeys had holes in all of the mountains,
And the iron men dropped the rails, and the section gangs
Had hooked them up, and the lever jerkers set the switches,
And the train delayers stacked up tickets and schedules,
And the tent stake drivers had no more nails to nail,
And the carnival crew banged all of the cars together,
And the car inspectors were smiling, and the yard masters
Were snoozing, and the paperweights had full ink barrels,
And the last handrail was shined up by the last porter,
And all the throttle pullers, fire eaters, ticket snatchers
And air givers said okay, the god-damn railway officials
Showed up in thousands and held a banquet in the firebox.
There she was in the daylight, the Eagle and her coaches,
Her boxcars, her flatcars, her tank cars, and her caboose:
The engineer and fireman couldn't climb up the gangway
Without carrying bedrolls, so they rode in a balloon
Up where the mules hauled coal out of the tender in cars
And unloaded it in front of the two-ton scoop shovel
By the fire door, with black coal flying into a white fire;
And pretty soon, when the safety valve showed a feather,
The engineer spit, tugged on his hat, and then cranked up
The four-barrel push-pull motor which drove the throttle.
As soon as the train was rattling, orders were written up
On rolls of newsprint, and stomped out in dot and dash
By square dancers in work boots. It was a big train:
The high-pressure cylinder couldn't be walked in a week,
Smoke took a month to float to the top of the stack,
And the wheel made one revolution between paydays.
The Eagle was so long a streamliner the conductor
Had to ride toward the glory wagon on a race horse
And punch tickets by shooting holes with a forty-five.
They'd dish out a whole cow for a steak in the chow car,
Hoist spuds on crane hooks, mix gravy in real boats,
And pump the coffee and moo juice from a tank car.
When the new hogger honked the new whistle the steam
Clouds busted and it rained too much, but the big bitch
Was the headlight, which lit up the farms for eight hours

After the train was gone, and the hay pitchers were hot:
It singed the wheat, it dried the ditches, and it kept
The gosh-darn chickens up till all hours; when the hogger
Bolted six-inch iron plate over it, it shined right through,
And so he crashed out the reflector, yanked all the wires
Out of the sockets, and took a hammer to the dynamo,
Which cut the light's range down to a mile and a half.
Cal, of course, was all for motion, and one July morning
He got an idea of the Eagle at a real healthy speed
On a hill-country run, when the up-and-down slopes
Boosted her like mathematics; the hogger got cautious
And whistled for the brakes, but it was like the brakemen
Were dozing or something, because she just cracked on,
And when all that tooting didn't wake up the boomers
It scared the engineer, who hauled on the reverse stick
With his arms and legs, till he stuck it in the corner:
Now, it turns out the Eagle was barreling so fast
The whistle's whistle was blowing by her crew before
They had a chance to hear it: she had to roll backwards
Till they caught up with the squawk, and when she came
To a full stop she was still doing sixty miles an hour.
In not too long, they were so far ahead of schedule
They were rolling in an hour before they left the station,
And so old speed-crazy Cal handed his star engineer,
Armstrong, a pair of goggles a foot thick, and said
Go double speed, which was no sweat, since all this time
Nobody had opened the throttle beyond the third notch.
The train boomed by the one-horse towns, mixing up
The slickers, by the fat farms, stacking hay, shucking corn,
Across the lie-down rivers and the stand-up mountains,
It moved into the big sticks, on its last go-around,
In and out of the weather, the sunlight sparking off it,
When Cal yelled okay, eagle eye, give her all she's got;
And speed ain't the word for it when she was wide open:
In back the rails were puddles and the crossties smoke,
Out the window was just a red, white and blue blur,
And when they were highballing too fast for map reading
They hit a long uphill mile, and boys, it was the end
Of the Ireland, Jerusalem, Australia, and Southern Michigan
Railroad; at the very top the Eagle slipped off the earth,
Out of gravity, into the blue: yeah, but I hear it's still
Chugging between stars, on the Aldebaran to Orion line.'

9

'Howdy, partner! Oh man. Shove it, Red Jack; I'm sleeping.
I'll be a bobtail rooster! I ain't seen you since morning.
Of all the! What is this, your birthday? Get out of bed!
What's up? Oh, nothing! Don't kid your grandma. Okay,
It's a bull dance. What, in the shanty? I'll kiss a cow!
Is it rolling? Yeah, it's rolling, and I don't mean maybe!
Give me an idea. Who's whooping it up? Paul Bunyan.
It's a scrape, it's a jubilee! Come on, for heaven's sake.
I'm coming, I'm coming. It's high time, Rocky Dan.
Good god! Who's playing? I think it's, oh gee, let's see;
Old Lefty's scraping a horse's tail over a cat's guts,
I mean fiddling. Hey, I'm sorry, I was all worn out.
Skip it, friend; nobody hurt. I'll bet you Brimstone Bill's
On the dulcimer! He's wild. Here we are: oh, look there;
It's Big Swede and his North Sea piano! Squeeze it, man!
Let's wrestle, darling! I'm from Missouri: show me!
Ha, you waltz like a mule! Thank you. Your cider, buster!
Swing me! Is this a jig or a breakdown? Don't ask!
I can buck and wing, woops! Where'd my glass go? Hold it.
Okay, greenhorns: here's to tight cunts and easy boots!
Here, have a swallow. Mister, I'll have a whoopee cocktail.
My stars! Hey, they're playing Flat River Gal, my favorite!
It's the gospel, honest! Hand me the barrel, I'm thirsty.
Give this man a cigar! It won't wash, Pumphandle Joe.
No fooling, now! You're funny. I am, huh? I'll funny you!
I'm giving you the straight of it, and you won't buy it?
Here's looking at you, dreamboat. Look, it ain't the straight
Of it, it's the horse crap of it. Yeah, it's barefoot weather.
You're a bad actor. What? I look bad, but I feel good.
You're a fake, and a liar! Oh brother. Oh well, it's all
In a day's work. There ain't no such animal, period.
Oh yeah? Here I come, honey. I'll tell you what, big mouth.
Will you quit hogging the applejack? I like your nerve:
You're bold as anything, and you've got grit. Ups-a-daisy!
Good luck, because first I'm writing your mom a letter.
Don't look at me, question mark! I wake up like a goose
In a new world every day. I don't know from nothing. Yeah,
And then I'm knocking you into the middle of next week.
Now hold on, one minute! How are you fixed for moisture?
Oh I've got plenty. Whoa: nobody touches Slabwood Johnson,
And goes on breathing. Pardon me. I've got to see a Chinaman

About a music lesson. Now, now! Say hi to Lulu for me!
Hold her, deacon: she's headed for the barn! They don't come
Too tough for me! Says who? Say your prayers, little boy!
The first hundred years are the hardest. Says me! Okay if
I take notes? Oh, don't get hot. Break it up, you baboons.
Go ahead. I was just joking. It's too many for me. Hey,
Billy the Bum! Welcome back: how are you, boss? Oh, fair
To piddling. I'm quitting! Why? The hotcakes are too round.
Aw, go way back in the woods and sit down. Good night!
I'm teasing: I'm going strong, like always. I'll be tomcatting
As soon as we close camp. And where are you boys pointed?
I'm steering for Burnside Street, Portland. It's close by!
I'm heading out for Sawdust Flats, Muskegon. And you?
Oh, Cedar Root Charley and I have our hearts set on
Haymarket Square, back in Bangor. I want a blow job
From all one hundred of Old Colorado's girls! Yahoo!
Well, I'm looking to beat up Silver Jack just one time.
On my birthday I'm sitting down in the Red Light Saloon,
And standing up three days later with empty pockets,
Or my name ain't Roaring Jim! I'm bowlegged for love:
Oh, I love it! I can smell the farmer's daughters from here!
I wonder if I should go crazy and get hitched, buy me
A little ranch, a big house, raise up a gaggle of kids?
Okay, but first you've got to get out of this shanty, pal:
Go on, try and squeeze past me, I'm a lumberjack!'
It was so all-time happy in there, the room was tilting;
It was steamy and musical, and in between the dances
The boys sprawled back, trading chatter, singing The Jam
On Gerry's Rocks, all hundred verses, inventing more,
While over on the rain barrel was a tight checker game
In which Old Lightheart had the bulge on Dynamite Jack.
It was all back talk by the wood stove, and after joshing
About crossing bedbugs with bobcats to get bedcats,
And the one-winged and hilltop-circling pinnacle grouse,
Whose feathers' color changed according to the season
And who was looking, Brimstone Bill and Big Swede jumped
All whooped up into the great American lying contest:
'Hush up, saw boss, and I'll take you back to the old days,
When everything was bigger: when I was a kid we sowed
An acre of land on which nothing popped up but a turnip,
But we lost our two hogs inside it, and found poor folks

Living under one leaf, it ain't no lie nor whore's dream.'
'I'm sure you're for real, bullwhacker; my goodness, yes!
When I was just a squirt, my daddy was the top man
At the iron works, where he built him a kettle so big
If a man dropped his hammer on Friday he didn't hear
It clang till Monday, and we boiled your turnip in it.'
'I swear you're the original windjammer, but I'm not
Stretching it when I say our trains back home can't
Carry hay or the cows along the track will eat it, and once
I was riding when they stopped for a cow, chased her off,
And stopped an hour later, when they caught up with the cow.'
'Oh gracious, that wasn't slow, that was an express:
I razzed our conductor once till we got in a big tangle,
Rolled off the train, I knocked him out, woke him up with
A hat full of water, we hopped on the caboose as friends,
I jumped off for the cap he lost, and still made it back.'
'You may be proud of your slow train, but I like action:
Like when I bake biscuits, I start out at the pump,
And when the first drip drops I pick and shuck the corn,
Grind it, whack kindling, light the fire, and grab salt, milk
And lard before the drop hits the bottom of the bucket.'
'Yeah, but why dawdle like that when you might hurry?
When I'm hungry, I just shoot me a buck, I skin it,
I dress it, hang it in the smokehouse, tug off my boots
And lie back and read through the latest Police Gazette
Before the dang bullet can come out of my shooting iron.'
It was hard to say who started up the game of poker,
It was all just plain stud and high-low, dealer's choice,
With a tough ante, in freeze-out style with nothing wild,
And, with the mixed luck, it looked like it'd last till sunup,
Or till Johnny Inkslinger shut up, whichever was first.
'I was run out of Oklahoma over a poker hand, boys,
And rode a long-ear mule out of the town of Crossroads
Clear to Hog Eye, Texas, where I tied up at the saloon:
I slouched in and ordered a whiskey and lemonade,
I believe it's called rattlebelly; I knocked it off
While looking at the bunch of lazybones and sodbusters,
And said, "It looks like rain." This old pioneer walked up,
Everybody staring, slapped me on my shoulder, and said,
"Stranger, did you know there's only two kinds of folks
Who predict Texas weather?" I confess I was stumped:

"Only two kinds, old-timer? Okay, what might they be?"
He answered with a deadpan, "Newcomers and damn fools."
Well, the joint went crazy; lord! it was solid laughter
And shouts of "You're sold, partner," and "Set up the shots:"
I smiled, I bought a round like a good horse, and when
The rowdydow was over, and the bar was buzzing, I said,
"I see you're right, grandpa, when you say there's just two
Kinds of folks who predict Texas weather, newcomers
And damn fools: why, there ain't no other kinds in Texas."
I could've been elected mayor, but I marched by them,
Headed for the whorehouse, knocked on number twenty-one,
And a whoopee girl yelled, "Who's there? I'm in the tub!"
"My name's Inkslinger; why don't you unlock this door?"
"I won't see any old stiff," she said, "How tall are you?"
"I'm six feet: open up." "How do you measure yourself?"
"From the crown of my sombrero to the spurs on my boots."
"How long are your arms, Inkslinger?" "Oh, forty inches."
"How do you measure them?" "Shoulder bone to finger tip:
Open up!" "Okay, but how long is your cock?" "Three inches."
"Mercy me, how do you measure that?" "From the floor.'"
Paul Bunyan swallowed all his fun water, and showed them
His timber dance, he won a jackpot on a bluff, and
Squatted on a log bench and looked into the old fire
In the iron stove for a long spell, till he stood up,
Rubbing his eyes, and stepped out into the blue night.
It was crazy, but he was like a white pine himself
With the wind in his head, and the dusk in his arms,
Out under a red sky, and all that was left of the sun
In the work yard: he stood in the sawdust and talked
To the new crescent like a sailboat up in the air:
'Oh moon, you give me goosebumps: I'm a daylight boy,
All I know's the world of sweat, and siestas bewilder me.
I wish the sun was always up; I'd be out logging
Now, but I guess that's that: there's nothing left but scrap
And the sequoias. I could hang around, but I'd just see
My boys all scatter like sparks on the Fourth of July:
I can't stop them, but I can't holiday, it ain't my style;
I'm clearing out, I'll just go and hug them once more.
I'm a veteran of all our mornings, and I'm loyal to them:
The early camps, with big mouths, show offs, wonder men,
All of the strong-arm tramps showing up out of nowhere,

The blowups, the jokes and bellyaches, the slams, the scuffles
And the beautiful fistfights, where we became pals backwards,
I can name the years for history by the insane weather
And the scrapes with animals and greenhorns, oh my land,
We've charged all over the American map like a railroad,
From the skid roads to the boom towns, and in nice circles,
And the air was always full of brags, cracks and comebacks,
Big lies and old lines, swear words, tall tales and sweet talk,
I sure loved it, but it's like it was only a day. Oh,
I can't tell my roughs goodbye, my heart's too watery;
I hope they hold up, but I don't know why: they're loggers,
They're solid as the Rockies, in shape like the Mississippi,
They like to swim with catfish and frolic with grizzlies,
Bald eagles sing to them; oh yeah, I'll see them around.
Why am I out yacking to the moon, like a screwball?
I'm shoving off; I'm not sleepy, and if I'm crowded
By all I've done, I'll be okay once I'm on a frontier.
I might be invisible tomorrow, but nobody should wonder
Where the hell I am: I'm in the United States, working.'
Old Paul lifted his ax to his shoulder and shouted
To the blue ox, who bounced over: back in the bull pen,
Shanty Boy, the tall talker, climbed on the deacon seat
To spout a story, and as the big lumberjack walked off
Into the uncertain pines, he just caught the beginning:
'Out of the wild North woods, in the thick of the timber
And through the twirling of the winter of the blue snow,
Within an inch of sunup, with the dream shift ending,
A man mountain, all hustle, all muscle and bull bones,
An easy winner, full of swagger, a walking earthquake,
A skyscraper, looking over the tallest American tree,
A smart apple, a wonder inventor, the sun's historian,
A cock-a-doodle hero, a hobo, loud, shrewd, brawling,
Rowdy, brash as the earth, stomping, big-hearted, raw,
Paul Bunyan lumbered and belly-laughed back at the stars.'

Acknowledgments

Thanks are due to the editors of *Northwest Review*, who first published pages from this poem, and *Margie*, who first published section 4.

Sources

1

'The Round River Drive.' James MacGillivray, Douglas Malloch, 1910, 1914

'Paul Bunyan in 1910.' Edward Tabor and Stith Thompson, 1910, 1946

'Legends of Paul Bunyan, Lumberjack.' Bernice Stewart and Homer Watt, 1916

Paul Bunyan. James Stevens, 1925

A Treasury of American Folklore. Edited by Bruce Botkin, 1944

Type and Motif-Index of the Folktales of England and North America. Ernest Baughman, 1966

2

Paul Bunyan and His Big Blue Ox. W. B. Laughead, 1914, 1922, 1934

Paul Bunyan. Esther Shepherd, 1924

The Saginaw Paul Bunyan. James Stevens, 1932

Ol' Paul. Glen Rounds, 1936

Paul Bunyan: The Work Giant. Ida Turney, 1941

The Wonderful Adventures of Paul Bunyan. Louis Untermeyer, 1946

Legends of Paul Bunyan. Edited by Harold Felton, 1947

They Knew Paul Bunyan. E. C. Beck, 1956

'The Making of a Myth.' P. M. Clepper, 1971

(Paul Bunyan: Last of the Frontier Demigods. Daniel Hoffman, 1983)

3

Songs of the Michigan Lumberjacks. E. C. Beck, 1942

Woods Words: A Comprehensive Dictionary of Loggers' Terms. Walter McCulloch, 1958

Wisconsin Lore: Antics and Anecdotes of Wisconsin People and Places. Robert Gard and L. G. Sorden, 1962

Timber! Toil and Trouble in the Big Woods. Ralph Andrews, 1968

4

American Humor: A Study of the National Character. Constance Rourke, 1931

Holy Old Mackinaw: A Natural History of the American Lumberjack. Stewart Holbrook, 1938

Davy Crockett: American Comic Legend. Anonymous, 1835-56, edited by Richard Dorson, 1939

Down in the Holler: A Gallery of Ozark Folk Speech. Vance Randolph and George Wilson, 1953

Reference

Hammond's New Supreme World Atlas. 1952

American Thesaurus of Slang. Second Edition, A Complete Reference Book of Colloquial Speech, edited by Lester Berrey and Melvin Van Den Bark, 1953

Hammond's Pictorial Travel Atlas of Scenic America. E. L. Jordan, 1955

The Folk Songs of North America. Edited by Alan Lomax, 1960

Roget's International Thesaurus. Third Edition, edited by Lester Berrey and Gordon Carruth, 1962

The Concise Oxford Dictionary of Current English. Based on The Oxford English Dictionary and Its Supplements. Sixth Edition, edited by J. B. Sykes, 1976